MAKE YOUR OWN MAGIC

MAKE YOUR OWN MAGIC

AND GET OUT OF YOUR OWN WAY

MADISON PALICA

MAKE YOUR OWN MAGIC

and Get Out of Your Own Way

ISBN   978-1-64137-351-7   *Paperback*

            978-1-64137-682-2   *Ebook*

CONTENTS

"You create your own reality."

—JANE ROBERTS

For Magic – the invisible yet tangible, the gentle yet powerful. I trust you will use this book as you wish, taking it exactly where it is needed.

INTRODUCTION:

___

"The sole motive which inspired me to write this book was a sincere desire to be helpful to others by sharing with them … the stupendous fortune which became mine the moment I discovered my 'other self.'"

—NAPOLEON HILL[1]

A successful man named Aubrey Drake Graham said in the year 2011, "You only live once, that's the motto … YOLO."

That really was my motto, especially because people thought that the world was ending in 2012. I *had* to live life to the absolute fullest or else I would never forgive myself.

___

1   Hill, Napoleon, Sharon L Lechter, Mark Victor Hansen, and Michael Bernard Beckwith. 2011. Outwitting The Devil.

I would do things just for the sake of being able to tell a story afterward. It was that motto that got me to step out of my comfort zone for the first time, and countless times after. Without "YOLO" I probably would have never done a number of stupid things that, sure enough, gave me great stories to tell.

Furthermore, without "YOLO" I probably never would have gotten a taste of the adrenaline that comes with doing things I was afraid of. It pushed me over the brink of fear and started to teach me that fear was a waste of time.

At this point in my life, only fifteen years old, I had no idea that I could do literally whatever I wanted to. I had been stuffed with the concept of a life where you:

- Go to school
- Go to college
- Work a job you probably hate to make money
- Get married
- Are hopefully able to afford raising a family
- Sit around taking care of them
- Retire on a beach at sixty-five, finally doing what you want to in life (assuming you make it this far)
- Then die

I, luckily, took "you only live once" very seriously until it lead me into Magical territory I could hardly believe existed—doing *what* I wanted, *when* I wanted. It was so radical. Saying "YOLO" and getting out of my comfort zone was the first time I pushed myself past fear to do things for stories and memories.

Drake's "6God"-sent guidance taught me that I could craft my experience to give myself the story or feeling I was looking for. This turned out to be more expansive and full of life-changing wisdom than could have ever been expected.

What's more, without "YOLO", I'm not sure I ever would've stepped out of the dreary and predictable path I thought everyone was destined to live. Now, I'm making my life into the Magic that I have always secretly dreamed of—crafting my own story, or legacy.

I hope for you to be able to do the same.

***

A book is an experience in text. I want this experience to be *for* you and *about* you. I want you to base all of these words off of you and your own life experience.

Make Your Own Magic holds lessons that I wish I could have had years ago during times when I was filled with confusion and panic.

I struggled growing up in a highly religious town and never quite fitting in. I moved to a different state all alone in hopes of finding my way. I experienced a culture shock, the crumbling of my life's foundation, and the questioning of everything I had ever known.

Anxiety plagued me while away from home. Making friends was hard for me to do, struggling to fit in yet again. I went through a faith crisis, as well as an extreme health crisis, and I ventured into territory I had never before been exposed to.

I dealt with loneliness and feelings of abandonment. People around me gaslighted me, and I often questioned my *own* sanity. Becoming secure with who I am as a person took years of diligent work, and it is something I am still working on every day.

In this book I will tell you the story of how I went through my own struggles, and how those dark times led me to the discovery of Magic.

This book's purpose is to help point *you* to the Magic that exists within us and alongside us—to help you empower yourself to live and love to the absolute fullest—without doing the years of research that I did.

***

I wish I would have known sooner the role that independent thought plays in a person's life. I had made so many unconscious decisions based on my previous social conditioning that led me to choose friends, partners, and even institutions that were not right for *me*.

I wish somebody would have told me that I have the God-given right to do and create absolutely anything I want in life. For too long I lived in survival mode, thinking that I was different, life was hard, and that I would never be able to support myself.

I wish I had a teacher to sit me down and tell me the truth of the connection between all things. I had believed that everything was separate—me from you, man from nature, religion from science, head from heart.

And I wish I would've known that the most Magical and helpful things in life are unseen, but that they really do exist. I wish I would have known that I hold Magic within me—we all do.

Change comes from within, where the Magic lies in waiting. As such, this book starts and ends with one person:

You.

Meet these words with an open mind and heart. Let the words and images fill you, and then decide how you feel about them. Everyone is different—do what feels right for you.

If something you read:

- Resonates with you
- Touches your nerves
- Gives you chills
- Makes you say "Whoa"

… then take that information, underline it or highlight it, and be sure to *remember it.*

However, if something I say does not hold weight to you, does not make sense, or makes you feel uncomfortable, that is OK. You can disregard it and keep reading, though I hope you do take note of the things that cause you unease and investigate why that might be.

Always love yourself, trust yourself, and have faith that life is your partner-in-crime. Life and your intuition are always

guiding you on your highest behalf, even in the dark times—
you need only learn to simply listen to its subtle communication. There is a lesson in every experience.

What you, the reader, do with this book is more important than what I teach through this book. You will all react
according to your own perceptions and experiences. Your
background is essential to how and what you learn here, and
I want you and your experiences to become the core of this
course on Magic.

This book is only a gentle facilitator along your life path.
I want to make sure you understand that it will not deliver
you Magic, but simply point you in Magic's direction and ask
you to find it for yourself.

You are the only person who knows what you dream of,
this book does not. You are here to make that dream
happen, to follow your love and your joy and your peace.
Nothing else.

And there is absolutely nobody stopping you from doing that
… but you.

Luckily, life has guided you to this book, which will help you
to get out of your way and to pursue and achieve your dreams.

There are about 130 million books in this world.[2] The fact that you've been drawn to this one, or perhaps it was carried to you, is no small coincidence.

That, my friend, is Magic.

***

Most adults probably have a hard time identifying just what Magic is, how it works, or how to make use of it. It's true that Magic is largely unseen, but there are times we get to experience it, like:

- Those times when coincidences happen that are so meaningful and perfectly-timed we call it "lucky," "fated," or "miraculous."
- Perhaps those occasions when something we have been thinking about materializes into our lives out of what seems like thin air.
- The moments when a sudden, ground-breaking epiphany just pops into our head as if out of nowhere, and leaves our perspectives forever changed.
- Even times when we wake up from a dream in which we were presented an idea or solution for a problem we have been facing in real life.

---

2   Parr, Ben. 2019. "Google: There Are 129,864,880 Books In The Entire World." Mashable.

These are all instances where real Magic is at play. And Magic is *always* surrounding us and guiding us.

People today are largely closed off to Magic because of society's need for conformity. Our imaginations have been shut off, in place of logic and rationality. An adult who even speaks of Magic likely gets called crazy, dismissed, or looked at with patronizing eyes.

But Magic wants nothing more than to help you; in fact, it is waiting patiently for you to interact with it and use it to your advantage. This book is about opening up your eyes and your heart to that Magic once again, the way you were open to it when you were a creative, fun-loving child.

This book will introduce you to:

- The perceptions that have shaped the fundamental aspects of your life story
- The idea that books contain Magic
- The concept of becoming the author of your own life story
- The collective narratives that are currently running in the world, and the dangers they carry
- A potential new narrative that relies on individual happiness and fulfillment
- Guidelines that put you in accordance with the laws of the universe

- The connecting points in this largely holistic, yet seemingly separate, world we live in
- Practical, personal, everyday advice for you to apply on mental, emotional, physical, and spiritual levels to help make your own life Magical

I believe these things are important for people to become aware of, because how can people be happy and successful in a world that they don't understand the true nature of? Better yet, how can people be happy and successful if they don't understand the true nature of *themselves*?

***

Depression and anxiety have made a home in 606 million people worldwide, according to the Anxiety and Depression Association of America.[3]

Suicide is the tenth leading cause of death in the US with 47,173 lives willingly taken in 2017 alone, according to the American Foundation for Suicide Prevention. That number pales in comparison to the estimated 1.4 million suicides that were attempted in 2017.[4]

---

3   "Facts & Statistics | Anxiety And Depression Association Of America, ADAA." 2019. Adaa.Org.
4   "The American Foundation For Suicide Prevention: Suicide Rate Is Up 3.7 Percent." 2019. AFSP.

The reality is, in a world that seems dark and downtrodden, we need hope. And in a world that increasingly feels like it has fewer and fewer places for us to turn, where do we go?

In college I went through my own phases of anxiety and depression, being prescribed anti-anxiety medication and just as quickly weaning myself off of it (I didn't like the research I was finding on its effects on the brain and body).

As I began to accept that the world wasn't going to give me the answers I was looking for and there weren't any places I could find handing them out, I had to try something else. I had to start down my own, unique path of far-reaching and holistic research.

The contents of this book all began as an internal experiment. I wanted to find Magic, a way to relieve myself of unhappiness and suffering. I wanted to prove to myself that Magic was real … and I *did*.

For years I spent my free time nose-deep in research, rather than hanging out with friends or having fun. I was trying to find the connecting points for all of these concepts that had been put in their own separate boxes—religion, science, health, psychology, history, and nature.

I was determined to find a way to bridge these seemingly separate things all together, to form a more holistic and unified view of myself and the world; something reliable and comprehensive that I could count on to make me truly feel better.

This book is meant to be exactly that comprehensive guide—a lifeline, a map, or a cypher, if you will. I wish for you not to just read this book, but to use it and apply it in all aspects of your life. That being said, I cannot promise results—every person is different, and this book may not be right for everyone.

Each word and lesson within this book came about due to my own crises, struggles, wounds, and failures. I wrote what I learned as I went through very real and very hard times. I wrote the things that gave me hope.

The energy and inspiration behind this book also came about by taking risks and experiencing times of euphoria. I followed my heart and listened to my intuition, even when people looked at me with crazy eyes, and it gave me a faith and confidence that I never possessed before.

The Magical journey I embarked on quickly brought me closer to not only myself, but also the world outside of me. I developed an empathy for others that I never quite felt before. When the world and I worked together to serve each other, it felt like what I could only explain as pure bliss.

I now feel very strongly that writing and sharing the information in this book is part of my life's purpose.

I want to wake people up to the Magic that is dancing right in front of them, inside of them, and just waiting to lend a helping hand. I want to help people learn how to use that Magic to their benefit. I want people to wake up to their true potential, to their own, unique loves, passions, and life purposes.

But I also want to start a ripple effect, beginning on a microscopic, personal level that will one day become tangible on a macro-scale, earth-changing level.

I want to *shift the direction of mass human consciousness,* for the benefit of ourselves, as well as all future generations.

PART I:

This part of the book introduces you to the foundations of a human being. It takes you through my personal story of building my foundation as a Mormon, and what it was like growing up in Utah. It relays just how that foundation fell through, then introduces you to the books that gave me hope after having my perceptual rug pulled out from under me— the first time in my life that I experienced Magic.

CHAPTER 1:

HUMAN FOUNDATIONS

"When people appear to be something other than good and decent, it is only because they are reacting to stress, pain, or the deprivation of basic human needs such as security, love, and self-esteem."

—ABRAHAM MASLOW[5]

Before I tell you my story, I must convey to you what a human foundation is.

All human beings are born incapable of caring for themselves. That is a skill we have to hope we are taught well. Or, we must

---

5   "Abraham Maslow Quote." 2019. A-Z Quotes.

try and fail ourselves until we learn how to do it correctly. This is a lifelong process.

As we age and mature, we work our way up a pyramid of human needs. You must, indeed, master each step of the pyramid before you can successfully move on to conquer the next. If you have not mastered the most fundamental of needs, you will not physically be able to achieve the things beyond them. Life can also set us back at any time, or wipe out our bases completely.

If you have not mastered the lower levels of the pyramid but reach for the top, you have shifted your focus before you are truly ready for it. In short, it is good to have goals—it is just not good to have goals so lofty that you can never reach them.

This is simply about taking baby steps.

Merriam-Webster defines a foundation as "a basis upon which something stands or is supported."[6] What can happen to a building with a weak foundation in the case of an earthquake? The entire structure may crumble.

Our foundations are our core needs, our roots that provide stability, our deepest beliefs and dearest belongings. Those

---

6   "Definition Of FOUNDATION." 2019. Merriam-Webster.Com.

roots are the foundation from which we build and construct ourselves and our lives.

So, if applied to humans with weak or unstable foundations, what could happen in the event that something shakes them? They may also crumble, just like the building.

***

Abraham Maslow, an American psychologist, conceptualized a basic pyramid of fundamental human needs:

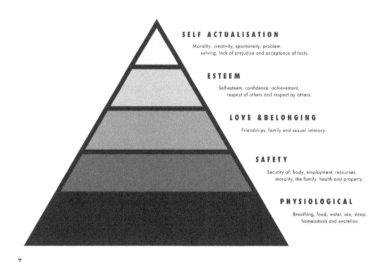

7

---

7   "Abraham Maslow's Hierarchy Of Needs." 2019. Medium.

1. PHYSIOLOGICAL NEEDS

Physiological needs make up the very base of human foundations. To simply live, a human being must have:

- Air
- Food
- Water
- Shelter
- Rest

A human who does not have proper access to any single one of those needs will have a slim chance of survival. They will have close to zero chance of ever pursuing the next step of Maslow's pyramid, or those beyond.

A lack of base physiological needs can result from a number of different things:

- Air pollution
- Water pollution
- Drought
- Lack of money
- Lack of resources
- Disabilities
- Natural disasters
- Wars

2. SAFETY

Safety includes, but is not limited to:

- Security of your own body
- Security of resources
- Safety of family
- Secure health
- Secure finances

Without a sense of safety and security to live within, one will be condemned to living a life in fear and insecurity.

A lack of safety could stem from:

- Abuse
- Manipulation
- War
- Institutional oppression
- Natural disasters
- Discrimination
- Physical/mental health decline

3. LOVE AND BELONGING

At this stage, a person seeks a deeper sense of connection that can be fulfilled with:

- Friendships
- Family relationships
- Romantic partners
- Intimacy
- Community

Overall, this step in the pyramid is about seeking a genuine sense of relation to other people—we are social creatures, and social contact is an important part of our healthy functioning.

Without sincere human connection, one may feel:

- Lonely
- Unhappy
- Isolated
- Lost
- Hurt
- Confused
- Stressed
- Depressed
- Anxious

The need for love, though always there, is especially strong in children. It can actually override children's need for safety.[8] If not fulfilled as a child, this need will carry through to adulthood. In this sense, it can possibly be harmful—many will continue to disregard safety in order to feel connection.

A lack of belonging can stem from:

- Neglect
- Social anxiety
- Isolation
- Lack of confidence
- Being shunned or ostracized

4. ESTEEM: EXTERNAL & INTERNAL

Maslow split this into two sub-categories: External esteem, and internal esteem.

External esteem includes:

- Respect
- Social status
- Recognition
- Validation

---

8   "Parents, Let's Talk About Maslow's Hierarchy Of Needs." 2019. Bluedollarbull.

- Approval
- Attention

These needs are also *egoic*—they form a sense of personal identity. One should not rely on external respect or status to fulfill this step. Generating esteem for yourself from within is important, as one may not be able to always be externally validated or accepted.

Internal esteem includes:

- Self-respect
- Confidence
- Achievement
- Attainment
- Competence

Without esteem, one will never gain a mindset or momentum strong enough to fully achieve their dreams and goals. There may be imbalances on this level that lead to an inferiority complex, or an uncertainty about oneself.

5. SELF-ACTUALIZATION & TRANSCENDENCE

Self-actualization and transcendence sit at the very tip of the pyramid. Self-actualization is described by Maslow as "becoming the most that one can be." At this stage, a person is free to explore:

- Creativity
- Spontaneity
- Morality
- Freedom

This may look different for each person, but can include:

- Acquiring a partner
- Getting married
- Becoming a parent
- Developing or projecting talents and abilities
- Getting that dream job
- Moving into your dream home

In his later years, Maslow seemed to have realized that the most full realization is, in fact, to give oneself to something *beyond* just themselves. He called that "transcendence." I believe this may be interchangeable with the term *enlightenment*. A transcendent person:

- Has reached the highest point of human consciousness
- Acts upon inclusion and connection

- Feels connection to other humans
- Includes other beings in their decisions
- Acts on behalf of the whole earth and the entire cosmos

To live in transcendence is to make your life an act of service and love on behalf of others that comes from being wholly fulfilled within yourself.[9]

***

In conclusion, these are the five bases of crucial human needs. To live the life of a fully-realized human, one must satisfy physiological needs, attain safety, feel love and belonging, gain esteem, and finally, self-actualize and serve others.

Maybe you have mostly mastered the steps of the pyramid but have a few holes here and there. Maybe you can directly pinpoint which step you are currently stuck at. Or maybe this is a wake-up call to stop pursuing things that are simply out of reach at this current moment.

Whatever stage you are at, you are OK where you are—do not put yourself down for not having the pyramid perfectly mastered. Now that you are aware of where in this pyramid you lie, you have already made the most important step toward

---

9   Mcleod, Saul. 2019. "Maslow's Hierarchy Of Needs." Simply Psychology.

attaining your goals—you have a starting point and a clear focus of where your attention should be directed.

This book will help guide you toward actualization and transcendence.

What amazes me is that only the first step of Maslow's hierarchy is completely physical. We definitely need real food to eat, water to drink, and air to breathe. But from safety and beyond, the steps can be physical *or perceptual.*

Safety, love, esteem, and actualization can be created by your mental world. This is not to say that physical safety is not important. Of course one does need physical safety. But the *sense* of safety, or lack thereof, can potentially be created by your mind with no basis in reality at all.

I remember a time when I was in bed with a friend during a sleepover. It was warm and cozy, the door was shut, the house was locked. My friend slept like an angel within this safe space, yet I lied there with eyes wide open. Though I was in a completely safe space, my mind was alert for danger and I was unable to close my eyes out of fear of an intruder.

I was at home and safe in my bed yet still scared, even in the clear absence of danger.

If I can think myself into false danger, then I also have the ability to think myself into feeling connected while experiencing disconnection, or feeling disconnected in the clear presence of connection. The other steps work the same way as well. Sometimes overthinking can be the sole cause of unhappiness.

Our pyramid, the basis of who we *think* we are and what we *think* of life, is buried *deep* in the subconscious mind. A foundation is a collection of old mental constructs that began to take form as a newborn. It consists of stories you have been told, even stories you tell yourself, all accumulated and hardened over the span of your lifetime: this is *conditioned programming.*

"A young child's daily experiences determine which brain connections will develop and ... last for a lifetime ... Children who experience more positive interactions in their early years go on to be healthier and more successful in school and life. Unfortunately, the opposite is true as well ..."[10]

Our programming begins when we are the most impressionable. A child's brain is 90 percent developed by the age of five, according to First Things First, a voter-initiated, statewide organization in Arizona that funds early education and

---

10   "Brain Development – First Things First." 2019. First Things First.

health programs.[11] Since our foundation is mostly built by the age of five, this also means the consequential internal experience of life is vastly different between individuals, even those experiencing similar things.

The core foundation to our pyramid of needs, therefore, begins as a result of our initial environment. We are reliant on our caretakers and social environment to make sure we develop properly in those five years, and this affects our behavior and abilities for the rest of our lives.

"The connections needed for many important, higher-level abilities like motivation, self-regulation, problem solving, and communication are formed in these early years—or not formed."[12] Many of us, unfortunately, grew up in negative childhood environments that may have inhibited our proper growth as adults.

A person who grew up with emotionally distant parents will more than likely struggle with connection for the rest of his life—because his brain was molded that way as a child. That child never learned how love or belonging works, so that step in the pyramid will be a life-long struggle unless re-taught how to properly connect with people.

---

11   Ibid.
12   Ibid.

***

Unfortunately, because the source of many internal issues are tucked away and hidden under years of added knowledge and experiences, these deep underlying beliefs and programmed behaviors can be hard to remember and discover.

Therapy and counseling can help get to the root of these traumas, events, memories, or experiences. It can also be difficult to process certain memories or events that affected you as a child once you have found them, but the healing process it sparks is incredibly worth it.

Finding conditioned beliefs that set in as children, as well as understanding or changing those beliefs, requires deep internal work. It is a lifelong process of healing and re-teaching yourself—but one that is worth all of the effort.

Dr. Nicole LePera, PhD, otherwise known as The Holistic Psychologist, says, "Healing is a lifelong journey. It is a choice to live life as a student. A practitioner. It's a choice to go past the conditioning, the emotional addictions, and the ego to create a version of self in line with who you actually are. It's unbelievable just how much of us is programming. It's shocking at how few of us actually have the skills needed to live a fulfilled life."[13]

She describes the process of treating conditioned programming as something that will "allow you to choose new beliefs in alignment with who you want to be rather than repeating narratives given to you in childhood." Some aspects in life these narratives affect include:

- What you look for in a partner
- Spirituality/Religion: What they mean and how they are practiced
- Where you live
- What career decisions you make
- Finances: What money means and how much you make/need
- How you express yourself: Hair, dress, how you speak, etc.[14]

Repeated narratives, whether voiced by your parents, your childhood school teachers or religious teachers, even your friends, literally become programmed into your brain. Timothy Leary, an American psychologist, said that, "if we don't take the responsibility for programming it, then it will be

---

13 Lepera, Nicole. 2019. "Things You'll Learn On A Healing Journey." Pictame.Com.
14 Ibid.

programmed unwittingly by accident or by the social environment."[15] Thoughts and stories solidify into something that you subsequently, and unconsciously, base your views and therefore your actions around.

The brain reacts to programming, mere mental constructions, and this is what you believe to be "you." But these programs are not you. This is only the makeup of the ego. "Ego is no more than identification with form, which primarily means thought forms ... and it has a relative, not an absolute reality," explains Eckhart Tolle.[16]

The more you reinforce each story or belief, the deeper that specific programming becomes engraved into your brain. That is to say, it becomes more strengthened and *real*, whether the story is true or false.

You create neural pathways with each thought, and these pathways make up 60 percent of your brain, according to D. Kacy Cullen, an associate professor of neurosurgery at the University of Pennsylvania.[17] Neural pathways play a large role in the way people perceive the world around them, as well as the way they perceive themselves individually.

---

15   "Timothy Leary Quote." 2019. Quotefancy.Com.
16   Tolle, Eckhart. 2015. A New Earth. London: Penguin.
17   "Brain Pathways, Explained." 2019. Youtube.

The more often you think something, the deeper that specific thought pathway becomes embedded into your brain—and the easier it becomes to think that thought repeatedly. You are then more likely to follow that path of thought, and it makes it harder to think outside of the box.

Think about this the next time you find yourself repeating automated phrases like, "I can't do this," or, "I'm not good enough," or, "I don't deserve that." The more you affirm these to yourself, the more they become your personal truth—whether based in reality or not.

To find that our foundation may be more mental than physical does not diminish its importance. It does, however, add a lot of flexibility. For, if a long enough amount of time passes without the use of certain, encoded pathways in our brain, there is a chance it can become dismantled, according to Dr. Kathie Nunley, who specializes in curriculum development and systemic change.[18]

If our foundations are mental, just thoughts that we have invested a lot of time and energy into, would that mean our beliefs are … imaginary?

---

18 Nunley, Kathie. 2019. "Dr. Kathie Nunley's Layered Curriculum Website For Educators." Help4teachers.Com.

Is it possible to make something seem real, simply by thinking a lot about it?

That can be scary to think about. If beliefs can be imaginary, that must mean we are wrong about some things we believe in. But, if so, that must also mean that we have a lot of flexibility in what we *choose* to believe, and therefore experience.

Mastering the steps of Maslow's pyramid may be as simple as perceiving things differently. Re-building a strong, sturdy, positive foundation can be as simple as changing the direction of your thoughts.

***

I think it is important for everyone to become aware of their perceptions, opinions and beliefs. I think everyone should question their learned foundations, and try to look at themselves and others from different perspectives. It is important because this is the only way for people to empower themselves fully and begin to live a life that they truly love and desire.

To realize that even the most painful memories are only existing now as thoughts in your head, and that you can stop thinking about them and acting them out at any time, is a declaration of freedom. You *can* free yourself from your past and from your mind.

There are likely certain people, events, and situations that you most identify with and that have become a part of your perceptual story. Perceptions, however, can often be distorted.

Learning that you have lived according to distorted perceptions can be hurtful or traumatic. Experiencing a hole being put into your beliefs or perceptions of yourself or your world, your foundation, can often feel like sinking.

Yet, the things you have built your perceptual sense of safety, security, and belonging out of are always at risk of withering away, or crumbling under weight. This can come about from a number of things:

- A tragic loss
- A major health scare
- Losing a job
- Going through a divorce
- Learning new information
- Moving to a new location
- A natural disaster
- Leaving a religion
- Living through a war

When a foundation gives out, your ego goes tumbling with it. Because many of us are completely identified with our ego, our sense of self, this tumble can be life-changing and terrifying.

Though a total foundation crumble can feel like a black hole, or a void, it is also the place of pure potential where you get to rebuild yourself and your life exactly the way you want from scratch.

***

To continue through this book, it is important to remember the five main pieces to every person's foundation:

- Physiological
- Safety
- Love/Belonging
- Esteem
- Actualization/Transcendence

Of those steps in the pyramid, the first is physical and the rest can be physical or perceptual. These foundations form almost completely by the age of five. We act according to what we learned in those early years for the rest of our lives.

Changing this programmed behavior can take a lot of internal work, but it helps us to heal and live more happily. When our foundations are shaken or challenged, it can feel like our world is collapsing, though only our ego is.

The collapse of the ego is not bad but necessary for your authentic self to begin to emerge. You can then build a sturdier foundation for yourself by cultivating awareness of your thoughts and thinking differently.

Personally, as somebody with my mind set on reaching the state of self-actualization and transcendence, I intended on mastering each step of the pyramid. So how and why, despite thinking my foundation was strong, did it begin to crumble and shake my whole world?

Simply by learning new information.

CHAPTER 2:

EARTHQUAKE

"If we have the truth, no harm can come from investigation. If we have not the truth, it ought to be harmed."

—PRESIDENT J. REUBEN CLARK, FIRST

PRESIDENCY, LDS CHURCH[19]

I was born and raised in Utah. Now, I know what you might be thinking … Mormons?

Yes. Mormons.

Provo, Utah, the area in which I spent most of my years, was recently ranked in a study by WalletHub, which said that,

---

19   Runnells, Jeremy. 2017. "CES Letter." Cesletter.Org.

"Out of 500 cities in the nation, Provo ranked dead last for diversity."[20]

My father converted to the Church of Jesus Christ of Latter-Day Saints (LDS). My mother never did join, though she supported him and attended services. Both my two older sisters and I were raised as members of the LDS church, all baptized at eight years old. The premise was that, once we were older, we could decide for ourselves whether we wanted to stay a part of the church.

Church members are generally kind, selfless people who take great care of themselves and are often talented and smart. I think it is important to explain that the LDS church is not just a set of religious beliefs. It is more like an entirely devoted lifestyle.

Every Mormon knows the way of a Mormon, the life you are destined (or expected) to live if you want to make it to the Celestial Kingdom in the afterlife. The LDS church describes the Celestial Kingdom as, "the highest of the three kingdoms of glory ... To inherit this gift, we must receive

20 Stauffer, McKenzie. 2019. "Provo Named Least Diverse City In America." KUTV.

the ordinances of salvation, keep the commandments, and repent of our sins."[21]

The teachings of the church may seem innocent enough, but the culture it creates here in Provo can be overwhelmingly rigid and unforgiving. We were expected to attend church each Sunday for three hours, hold a church-based family night on Mondays ("family home evening"), activities on Wednesdays, and camp in the summers. Most of us also attended "seminary," a religious class in our school schedules.

We did our best to follow the teachings, paid our tithing each month (10 percent of what we earn), drank no tea or coffee, dressed modestly, and said our daily prayers to the Heavenly Father. Many of my friends did not kiss or date until they were sixteen years old. There was little sign of drugs or alcohol, and sex was to be saved for after a special temple marriage to a fellow Mormon.

My foundation was built on what my family provided for me, and what the church taught as a way to "return to the Heavenly Father." So the church's values became my own.

This is how one might achieve Maslow's hierarchy of human needs as a Mormon in Provo, Utah:

21　"The Church Of Jesus Christ Of Latter-Day Saints." 2019. Churchofjesuschrist.Org.

1. PHYSIOLOGICAL

The base of my pyramid, my physiological needs, were largely provided for me by my parents and my environment—a blessing that many are not so fortunate to receive. For that, I am grateful. I assume most other Mormons in Provo are also provided their physiological needs by their environment, so we will move on to the next step.

2. SAFETY

Now, one can seek a sense of safety. Given our anti-diversity community, safety was not hard to find. I could compare my town to some sort of Utopia—almost all people are white and in the same LDS religion.

In fact, my area is commonly referred to as "Happy Valley," a nickname given to Utah County when 90 percent of the population were members of the LDS church.[22] Luke Hickman, a writer for a local university's news website, the *UVU Review*, says, "since then this appellation has been used positively and negatively to refer to the environment created by the morally stringent standards of the LDS church's members."[23]

---

22 Hickman, Luke. 2019. "Why It's Really Called Happy Valley". Uvureview.Com.
23 Ibid.

3. LOVE AND BELONGING

Social belonging comes naturally and at a young age, as you simply become friends with children of families that attend church in the same ward as you. You become well-adapted to the other kids in your class, and you are kept with your age group as you grow and move your way up through the church system. Many friendships and relationships for both children and parents are built and maintained this way.

4. ESTEEM

One can then seek esteem, both internal and external, by engaging in certain church-inspired events. Some of the most popular are:

- Getting baptized at eight years old
- Serving a two-year mission once out of high school
- Getting married in the LDS temple
- Having a large number of children
- Raising said children as LDS
- Repeat

5. SELF-ACTUALIZATION/TRANSCENDENCE

The self-actualization process often overlaps with ways of seeking esteem, as in acquiring a spouse or becoming a parent. One can also earn a pass to enter the beautiful, secretive temple. I have personally never been inside—even in the event of my sister's temple marriage.

Many may feel transcendent as they come to hold callings, or positions within the church, like the Priesthood. Others go on to become teachers, and some may even earn the privilege of becoming bishops—taking charge of an entire ward of people. All members in the ward report to the bishop for meetings and interviews.

***

As I grew up, I started to slowly become more aware of how I was personally affected by the LDS church and the culture it created. I started to feel guilt and shame from not following teachings directly, afraid that God had seen me mess up.

Kids would criticize me on the school bus for not being at the Wednesday activities, though I had dance practice on Wednesday nights. Glares could be felt at the pool when I was the only one wearing a bikini.

Adults began conversations with me by lines like, "So, I hear your mom isn't a member." My parents and I never thought that was very appropriate, but it was a common occurrence.

A neighbor even told a family friend of ours that my family and I were going down the wrong path. This was hurtful to me because, though we missed some church meetings or drank coffee, I felt my family and I were kind, generous, and moral.

Time went on and, as judgement from others seemingly increased, I began to feel more estranged from the church. I felt guilty that I lacked the spiritual connection it seemed all of my peers had. My desire to participate and abide by the church rules began to diminish in the face of this.

What bothered me most, though, was the judgement of my sweet mom—the "non-member."

She was met with what, to me, seemed like harassment from ward members and missionaries to get her to join the church. Somehow they got her to teach a church class once, even as a non-member. Yet, it felt as if she was still constantly looked down upon, as were my sisters and I for becoming less frequent visitors.

My mom grew up in the South where tank tops, coffee, and sweet tea were a part of daily life. She never quite liked the strict culture here in Utah. It seemed especially ironic that coffee and tea were banned for their caffeine contents, yet

LDS members were rapidly consuming Diet Coke and Mountain Dew.

As I aged and matured, my mother and I began to agree more on some of the hypocritical, ironic, or confusing teachings and behaviors of the church and its members. We did not like that we were ostracized for such simple things as what we chose to drink. Coffee and tea even have inherent health benefits!

The big hunch at the core of the LDS church teachings is that members, these kind and genuine people, are taught to disengage in social interaction with non-Mormons. Members are also instructed to never question the ever-changing teachings or words of the church or the living prophet, as he is "the mouth-piece for God."

This idea of obedience and division taught by the religion is further strengthened by spiritual worthiness interviews, which allow or deny a member access to the LDS temple. MormonThink, a website "concerned with truth," explains that, "Church officers make every effort to see that no unworthy person enters the house of the Lord."[24]

---

24 "Temple Recommend Interview Questions." 2019. Mormonthink. Com.

Question number seven in the spiritual worthiness interview reads: *"Do you support, affiliate with, or agree with any group or individual whose teachings or practices are contrary to or oppose those accepted by the Church of Jesus Christ of Latter-day Saints?"*[25]

And so it seemed that as I began to step away from the church and disregard its teachings, the people in my life that supposedly cared about me stepped away as well. It was especially isolating and hurtful to me as a young teen.

In middle school it seemed I lost many of my friends because of my disobedience to church rules. It seemed that the parents of my peers, who attended church together in the same wards, came to the conclusion that I was a "bad girl." Subsequently, many of my friends were instructed to stop spending time with me.

I never quite understood what I did wrong in order to receive such harsh punishment. It broke my heart, especially when rumors would arise. But in hindsight, it seems my peers were only doing as they thought they should in order to be up to par with the church's standards.

---

25   Ibid.

I wondered to myself, *Why does religious status matter more than friendships?*

I questioned how people could, even if unconsciously, use church teachings as a tool for division, especially among their children. How could that be, if the church was supposedly teaching love and forgiveness?

This is when I began to question the church entirely, therefore putting nearly my whole foundation at risk of collapse.

***

I started to consciously notice the strict control of lifestyle as well as judgmental behavior the teachings rendered. It became easy to see the pattern that the Mormon lifestyle urged you to repeat—get baptized, go on a mission, come home and get married, have lots of babies. It was at work everywhere I looked!

All the while, I knew the church was gathering money from each member of its population. With more research, I discovered my tax-exempt church was "likely worth $40 billion today and collects as much as $8 billion in tithing each year."[26]

---

26 "The Money Behind The Mormon Message." 2012. The Salt Lake Tribune

I learned the LDS church was also using its money in questionable ways.

The article mentioned one noteworthy investment: A megamall. "Built for about $2 billion, the City Creek Center stands across the street from the faith's iconic Salt Lake Temple."[27]

Something just didn't feel right about it all any longer.

As I searched for answers to my growing number of questions, my awareness grew more expansive. My foundation also grew weaker with each Google search.

Toward the end of high school I began to realize that I had been putting all of my faith in a God who was taught to be a passer of judgement. Wouldn't judgement be the complete opposite of unconditional love?

And wasn't God supposed to love unconditionally?

It finally dawned on me how frequently I had been succumbing to guilt, shame, fear, and praying for forgiveness from my God. In all honesty, I was afraid of Him and what he thought of me.

---

27 Ibid.

One day I came across an old journal entry I had written in my early teens. In it, I spoke of how I felt so guilty about a certain romantic event. Looking back, it was clear to see how innocent this event truly was, but I couldn't see that at the time I wrote it.

My written words shocked me and made me so sad for my young self. I wrote that I had repented and prayed to God for forgiveness, but I still felt as if God hadn't forgiven me. The writing said how I felt like I would never be good enough, and that I couldn't possibly be pure enough or Christ-like enough to live again in heaven one day.

There were even mentions of turning to drugs, or committing suicide. All of this as a young, innocent girl, over an equally innocent event.

Today, Mormon suicide rates are climbing. A report by *KUTV*, a Utah news source, says that suicide is now the leading cause of death for Utah teens between the ages of eleven and seventeen. The youth suicide rate tripled in Utah since 2007, "an alarming increase not seen anywhere else in the country."[28]

Ellen Degeneres suggested on *The Ellen Show* in 2018 that the shame caused by LDS church teachings may be a factor

---

28 Hatch, Heidi. 2019. "Utah Youth Suicide Now Leading Cause Of Death For Utah Kids Ages 11-17." KUTV.

in the leaping suicide rates. Ellen stated that, "Suicide in Utah has increased 141 percent because of the shame they feel from the Mormon Church." *Deseret News*, Utah's oldest daily newspaper, responded quickly by saying Ellen's claim was not backed by research.[29]

Whether Ellen was backed by evidence or not, I knew I had to leave the church and its culture behind. With as many questions that were running through my head, the one thing I knew was that I could never let myself fall into the pattern of the Mormon lifestyle—the *trap*. It seemed like nobody ever left my town.

Therefore, I decided to go out of state for college on not much more than a whim—my chance to run away and get a taste of the real world, outside of my "Happy Valley" bubble. And just like that I was preparing to head to a private university in Texas in a few short months.

The yearning to go my own way in life was strong, but so was a similar yearning to find truth in the church that I had once truly believed in. I was on a search for my own LDS testimony without the help of missionaries or other church members. I wanted to find out if the church's teaching were real, and to connect with a spirituality on my own terms.

---

29   "Op-Ed: Responding To Ellen On Mormons And Teen Suicide." 2019. Deseret News.

***

Arriving in Texas, at what I thought was a Christian university, I was greeted with a general drunkenness. When people heard I was from Utah, they usually asked if I had two or more moms (that's Polygamy). Time went on and people continually treated me as if I were an alien, both for growing up Mormon and for not wanting to join in on the partying.

Truthfully, I initially held a strong dislike for my new peers regarding, what I then perceived to be, their clear lack of morals—though most still identified as Christian. I did not want to be friends with people who could get hammered drunk three times a week or let strangers into their bedroom while intoxicated. These same people would then show up at their church on Sunday, which was held inside of a bar.

Initially disgusted by the hypocrisy of it all, which I was already all too familiar with, I found my new sense of comfort in a boyfriend who was from the other side of the country. We started seeing each other, partly because it was easy to always be around one another—we had a class together and lived in the same dorm. We also got along well, though we were fundamentally different.

He was very liberal, a stark contrast from what I was used to growing up in a *Fox News*-only household. Though I do credit him for rounding my edges, there was only one way for him to open up my mind to new information: crumbling the current foundation from which my life and myself had been built.

He took on the task of shattering all the rigid beliefs that I had cemented in place, until there was nothing left. He brought me to emptiness, the space full of nothing but potential.

That was undoubtedly painful, but he did it—and it was worth it.

My attendance at church did not last long in Texas. I went maybe three times, taking him with me to one of them. Sundays quickly gave way to lounging with him, giving into "temptation."

He was an intellectual, and pressed me on topics that the LDS church historically took a stand against—topics that now were in the heat of social debate, like gay marriage. I, of course, sided with what I knew from the church: to act on being gay was a sin.

He pressed me harder, looking for reasons that *I* believed in, not just what the church had "brainwashed" me with. My brain was scrambling and I was terrified. As badly as I wanted something to prove I was right, I couldn't find a thing inside of me to come up with a logical reason why same-sex marriage was wrong.

All I knew was what the church had told me.

At the end of the discussion, I had to admit that gay people were just human and deserved love as much as any of the rest of us. It was so simple, so easy to see, once given a different perspective. Of course humans deserved to pursue love, no matter which way they happened to feel it.

My boyfriend and I had many of these different discussions, but that was the one that really did me in. My core of belief, or should I say my early mental programming and social conditioning, turned to ash.

I couldn't deny that my beliefs may have deserved to go up in flame, though. The church that I had followed so intently for so many years was truly teaching hate, judgement, and division.

With my beliefs punctured and no perceptual foundation or sense of self left, the world went on around me, but I felt empty inside. I didn't know what was right, or what to do. I didn't know what, or who, to believe.

My boyfriend was now the cause of my pain, yet my safety blanket. I had hardly any friends in Texas by this point, and my family was states away, unaware of the faith crisis I was experiencing.

I wondered, *How could the church be so wrong, so mean?* I didn't understand any of it.

It hit me hardest one day in Chili's when my boyfriend said, "Maddie, deep down we both know you're unhappy." I didn't know what to say. I didn't want to agree, but I knew that I did.

Though the church had caused me pain and I could clearly see where it was causing others harm, a part of me still wanted it to be true. For if it was not … that would mean I had been *living my entire life thus far as a lie.*

My ego had been wounded, and I had no sense of self to fall back on. I had no idea who I was anymore. What I didn't yet know was that exact point of emptiness was the blank canvas I *needed* in order to start anew.

It was then that I had to choose a certain course of action:

Continue to search for my testimony of LDS truth, or start over completely from ground zero?

CHAPTER 3:

BOOK MAGIC

"They have reared libraries in city, town … and have filled them with books giving to all who read a complete outline of the most useful knowledge mankind has gathered from his experiences."

—NAPOLEON HILL[30]

I once had a friend poke fun at me for the way I read books. He told me that I never just read a book, I make it a life-altering journey. Well, it's true. I can only read one book at a time and I give it my full attention and dedication.

I believe that books contain Magic.

---

30 Hill, Napoleon, Sharon L Lechter, Mark Victor Hansen, and Michael Bernard Beckwith. 2011. Outwitting The Devil.

And if you use the Magic from books in the right way, it will spill right off the pages and make your entire world sparkle. I think that is what the authors probably intend to happen, at least. What a wonderful thing it is to make imagination reality.

Book Magic also holds a subtle form of self-improvement. Naturally, I take that very seriously. Why wouldn't I want to be better?

Self-exploration, self-discovery, and self-improvement, I believe, are the most important things for every single human being on this Earth to do. Napoleon Hill in his book *Outwitting the Devil* said, "The first duty of every human being is to himself ... Beyond this, if one has time and energy not needed in the fulfillment of his own desires, one may assume responsibility for helping others."

The idea of life seems to be that we learn from our individual lessons and go on with an improved idea of how to reach our goals. Books are the Magic that keep a record of those lessons, helping the people who give warmth, presence, and movement to their pages.

Though the *Book of Mormon* was never a book I felt particularly drawn to, my world was still filtered by the cultural lens of religion while growing up. As a result, there were parts of my own human nature that I consequently only knew as sinister, and to act on them would be considered a sin.

Quite natural things, like sexual attractions or individual expression, had been painted in the light of the devil and I continually denied my own thoughts or feelings. I felt guilt and shame for having certain ideas or emotions in the first place and, as a result, I repressed certain aspects of myself for years.

Through my life-altering book journeys, however, I learned the beauty of contrast. Following the Magic contained in books I *was* drawn to, I discovered that meeting my own perceived shadow with a flicker of light could be an extraordinary, even spiritual, experience.

In order to feel happy, whole, and confident in who I was, I knew I could not continue to repress or deny any parts of myself—darkness included.

***

Before I had any idea of the power of book Magic, though, I was a typical senior in high school. I was skipping nearly all of my classes due to a very serious case of Senioritis. I only attended classes led by teachers I actually respected.

My English teacher was one of the few. In class, he had assigned us all to read one book—we got to pick any one we wanted from our library on one term: *It must be a classic.* Despite the fact that even the thought of reading a classic bored me, I respected the teacher, so I went along with it.

Lazily, I grazed over the books, waiting for one to really jump out at me. Much to my surprise, one of them did.

THE SECRET GARDEN BY FRANCIS HODGSON BURNETT

I remembered having seen some of *The Secret Garden* screen-play on TV as a child and I harbored an inner love of gardens, hidden pathways, flowers, and landscapes as a result of it. I knew this was the book that I didn't know I was looking for.

What I had never expected to get from reading this book, a children's classic, was the deep philosophical concepts woven into the conversations of the characters. I loved how easily the author portrayed the children, Mary and Dickon, as playfully wise. They wielded a wisdom that adults, for whatever reason, didn't seem to carry around with them anymore.

The children in *The Secret Garden* called that lighthearted, invisible wisdom *"Magic,"* with a capital "M".

As a kid I, too, felt entranced by magic for a certain period of time. I would learn card tricks, look at optical illusions, stay up late to order magic kits from infomercials … Now, here I was, about to graduate high school, and my inner child clung to the idea of magic once again.

I made it my secret journey to find the true source of the Magic these children talked of—to know for myself if it was real and to prove its existence. I knew Frances Hodgson Burnett was clever, and had surely inserted bits of it into her stories, so I found her pieces of "hidden Magic" in *The Secret Garden* and saved them forever.

A few quotes have stuck with me since then. I loved them because of the simplicity yet outrageousness they carried. It was almost radical to be calling something so small, so fleeting, Magic.

> "Of course there must be lots of Magic in the world …
> but people don't know what it is like or how to make
> it. Perhaps the beginning is just to say nice things are
> going to happen until you make them happen. I am
> going to try and experiment."[31]

Did Burnett mean to say that mere people could make Magic?

31   Burnett, Frances Hodgson. 2000. The Secret Garden. South Bend: Infomotions, Inc.

"Surprising things can happen to any one who, when a disagreeable or discouraged thought comes into his mind, just has the sense to remember in time and push it out by putting in an agreeable determinedly courageous one. Two things cannot be in one place."

I guess she did—as long the people are thinking the right way.

"If you look the right way, you can see that the whole world is a garden."

It was with that last quote in mind that I embarked on my *own* experiment to use Burnett's thought-Magic in my own way. From then on, life would be nothing but my own garden.

This life experiment was actually what gave me the boost I needed to leave Utah for college on my own. I went off to school confidently with my rose-colored lenses on and had never expected to come into contact with thorns. Clearly, the garden I had let myself into in Texas seemed wild, unpruned, and untamed. It was thick and unruly, like a maze, and I seemed to have lost my way inside of it.

But it was still a garden, nonetheless.

As hard as things got my freshman year of school, with my foundation now turned to dust, I never did waver in my life experiment for Magic. Since I had started replacing my negative thoughts with better ones, like the book suggested, I actually *had* been noticing a difference in life.

I knew that difference had to be a glimmer of the Magic: It was showing me that all the world could be my own optical illusion—it was whatever *I* made of it. Of course, optical illusion or not, there was no denying that I had some very real decisions to make about how I was going to continue with my life from this point of internal crisis.

***

The summer of my sophomore year of college I became near-desperate, still unsure of what to believe. The simplicity of "thinking positively" helped me in so many ways, but it wasn't quite cutting it for me anymore. Anxiety, tension, and nervousness became feelings I was experiencing more and more frequently.

I debated reading the *Book of Mormon*, in search of guidance. Instead, though, I lead myself into territory I hadn't yet ventured: mindfulness.

At the time, I knew nothing about mindfulness—if it worked, if it was real, or what that term even meant. What I *did* know was that it was time that I needed to let another book into my life, hopefully with newer Magic. Luckily, life easily led me to a book, teaching me about what a Magician mindfulness can be.

A NEW EARTH BY ECKHART TOLLE

Tolle is a contemporary spiritual teacher. The concepts he had written were hard to understand at first, but I was ecstatic. He, too, spoke of the power of thoughts—I felt like I was onto something.

I first read Tolle's The Power of Now, which taught me an important mental practice.

> "Try a little experiment. Close your eyes and say to yourself: 'I wonder what my next thought is going to be.' Then become very alert and wait for the next thought. Be like a cat watching a mouse hole. What thought is going to come out of the mouse hole? Try it now."[32]

It was quickly and actively changing my entire life from the inside-out. And I could feel it! I immediately scooped up his next book, A New Earth, which is powerfully transformative.

---

32 Tolle, Eckhart. 1997. The Power Of Now.

Never before had I so excitedly, yet peacefully, listened to my breath or looked at a bee on a flower. My mind stopped racing, and the *now*, the present moment, was something I started to genuinely enjoy.

> "That is the joy of being ... You can only feel it when you get out of your head. Being must be felt. It can't be thought."[33]

I had never understood before this book that *I* am not *my thoughts*. Tolle taught me that I am not the content of my mind, but rather the space that allows thought to arise. I am the constant presence in the background which notices my thoughts.

That shift in perception alone changed my life.

Practicing simply becoming aware of the hamster on the wheel that was my thoughts in my head, I wondered what it was I could possibly be thinking about non-stop. I quickly discovered that most thoughts were repetitive and not very pleasant.

I started to realize that my thinking never ended. In fact, now that I was actively noticing it, my thinking was kind

---

33   Tolle, Eckhart. 2005. A New Earth. London: Penguin.

of exhausting. At times it felt Magical, and other times I was confronted with personal shadows—my ego, in Tolle's words.

I became conscious of my thoughts, words, and actions even in times when I let my emotions get the best of me. I often witnessed myself saying or doing things I did not feel good about. But at least now I had the awareness of things I did not like, so that I could change them.

Before this, I had fully identified with my ego and it had been coming out when I didn't realize it. It had been a part of me, yet invisible to my untrained eyes.

At times I attempted to cast off my darkness and pretend it didn't exist. But I can tell you that it has done me more harm than good to try and deny my "evil twin." The ego is not something to hide from—while initially daunting, it can become an amazing mentor.

Every person has their own shadow. Society judges the shadow harshly, labeling it as bad, evil, or something to be ashamed of. *A New Earth* taught me that *it is not.*

A sense of peace crept into my life as a result of that book. My life experiment now included not just thought, but the total transcendence of it—*presence.*

I no longer felt the need to *filter* the world through my rose-colored lenses. I started to understand that roses come with thorns, and that thorns aren't bad, they are a different type of beauty. Only my thoughts could make a thing decidedly good or bad, anyway.

Life became saturated with a sense of Spirit for the first time in my nineteen years—and *completely without religion.* By this point, there was an itch inside of me that told me books really could be Magic—the real kind. And what's more, it seemed I was finding and using the Magic all by myself! I was attracting the Magic to me, like a magnet in a sense.

What were the odds, really, that the *very first books* I chose to read would change my life in such a profound way? Maybe *I* was Magic, even. I decided early on to not discount that thought.

The world became new and interesting to me, and I started to see things in a way that I never had before. Connections, patterns, and coincidences began to jump out at me. I became curious, light-hearted, and full of wonder—like a child again.

Not unlike the children I had read about in *The Secret Garden.*

Books then became my lifeline, which helped me to finally become *my own* lifeline. After *A New Earth*, another book quickly took me down the rabbit hole.

***

THE SECRET NATURE OF MATTER BY RICHARD GORDON

Gordon developed his own energy healing method, Quantum-Touch, which has been clinically tested and endorsed by the American Holistic Health Association.[34]

Mr. Gordon asked me:

> "Do our thoughts affect the outer world? Most people believe that our thoughts have absolutely no effect or influence on matter. And anyone believing otherwise is often accused of using 'magical thinking.' Children seem to innately believe in magic, whereas adults are taught to be practical and realistic … What actually happens when we project our thoughts, feelings, and energy? Is it all in our head, or is there something more going on?"[35]

---

34 "Richard Gordon." 2019. Amazon.Com
35 Gordon, Richard. 2017. The Secret Nature Of Matter.

Through his book, I started to become conscious of the fundamental building blocks of life—thoughts, feelings, energy, and matter. What's more, he found a way to connect them all.

Gordon taught me that "the observer affects the observed." This was to say that thoughts don't just run in one's own head and affect only the thinker, but that thoughts have a tangible effect on the things observed and thought *about*.

He taught me about Dr. William A. Tiller, a Stanford University professor, whose experiments "have repeatedly shown that the human mind can indeed have a direct impact on physical matter."[36] Tiller demonstrated that intention, or focused thinking, caused fruit flies to grow 15 percent faster than normal.

Tiller "suggested that consciousness and the phenomena observed are not limited by distance or time." The book taught me about *quantum entanglement*, the idea that two particles can become linked by thought and how, even if a billion light years apart, what happens to one particle immediately happens to the other.

---

36   Ibid.

The entangled particles always react, regardless of space or time. Einstein called this, "Spooky action at a distance."[37]

It was measurable Magic, discovered and documented by quantum physicists! I never would have believed that Magic and science could coincide—yet here was proof. Gordon assured me that most quantum physicists are baffled by their own discoveries on the intricacies of thought and matter, as they make us question all of our previous beliefs about reality.

Gordon confirmed to me scientifically what Tolle had taught me spiritually: that we are spiritual beings living a human experience. After all, "Physicists tell us that matter is 99.99999999934 percent empty space."[38]

I knew now that my thoughts weren't necessarily contained within my own head, but that they played a larger role in the world around me. This meant I could work Magic on more than just myself—I could use it to affect the world for the better.

***

---

37   Ibid.
38   Ibid.

A short time later, during the worsening of a health struggle that began in middle school (and that I am still learning to work with and heal), a doctor pointed me to a new book:

THYROID HEALING BY ANTHONY WILLIAMS

He was a "medical medium." He said he had a voice in his head that told him what to write. Mr. William was able to have conversations with what he deemed "Spirit."

And that Spirit had not only spotted his Grandma's lung cancer when he was a child, but had gone on to help him publish multiple books on health and healing. Together, they have changed the lives of millions—though William is now criticized for "magical thinking" permeating his writing by logical adults, just as Mr. Gordon had suggested was common.

Anthony William was *actually* Magic. But the book got me to realize that not only was the author Magic—all of our bodies are part of the Magic, too.

He said, in regards to people suffering in health and experiencing uncomfortable symptoms:

"I know those symptoms are difficult to deal with. Take heart that they're signs your body is helping you, because remember: Our bodies work for us. They protect us. They love us unconditionally."

He was the first person who ever taught me that my body "feeling wrong" was actually my body attempting to become right again. William enlightened me to the idea that our bodies are running with an intelligence incomprehensible to our little minds. If we tried to keep our body running with pure intellect, we would crash and burn.

And what's more, it lined up perfectly with what Gordon had already taught me, that

> "our intellectual capacity is eclipsed by the intelligence of a single cell which carries out thousands of chemical activities every second … All our cells are involved in respiration, digestion, elimination, cell division, and self-healing every second of our lives. The cells are even capable of repairing damaged DNA. The point is that it is not our intellect performing these miraculous activities … I suggest that this function is being carried out by spiritual intelligence."[39]

---

39   Ibid.

William also taught me about the true causes of illness as well as how to simply use *food* to heal myself—a comforting solution I had never been presented to by doctors.

This new perspective on my body, the flesh and bones that I will be caged in for my entire life, completely changed my perception of myself. The *Medical Medium* book exposed me to another Magic that had been hiding right under my nose my whole life—one that belonged to me. I developed a new, more intimate love for my body than I had ever felt before.

My body was its own Magically intelligent system, working constantly to keep me alive.

***

At this point in life, now enacting the healing diet William taught me, I felt as if I ruled the world. I felt like I had finally done it—finally reached the point of transcendence. I was:

- Taking great care of my body
- Eating healthy
- Tending to the garden in my mind
- Aware of the effect of my thoughts on the world around me
- Living in peace, presence, and self-empowerment
- Serving others however I could

Life felt like a dream. I thought that I had found and understood Magic, and therefore knew everything there was to know. I was fearless.

Life seemed as if it would encourage me, leave me hints, and give me meaningful coincidences—synchronicities, as Carl Jung posed.[40] It repeatedly felt as if fate would tap my shoulder and we would laugh together in nirvana.

This is enlightenment, I supposed. I trusted life as much as I trusted myself, so I never questioned where it took me. It then brought me to another book, one that would dampen the high I was feeling.

ISHMAEL BY DANIEL QUINN

It was recommended by a friend and gave me a shock I don't think I ever could have fully prepared for. Before being published, this novel received from Ted Turner, founder of CNN, the Turner Tomorrow Fellowship Award, worth $500,000. It is awarded to unpublished works of fiction offering creative and positive solutions to global problems.[41]

---

40 "Synchronicity." 2019. En.Wikipedia.Org.
41 "Readishmael.Com – Ishmael By Daniel Quinn Wins Ted Turner's Tomorrow Fellowship." 2019. Readishmael.Com.

A stranger once stopped me in the airport as I was reading it to tell me how important this book was—another synchronicity. *Everybody needs to read this important book.*

Daniel Quinn taught me about society at large:

"Mother Culture, whose voice has been in your ear since the day of your birth, has given you an explanation of *how things came to be this way.* Two different stories have been enacted here during the lifetime of man. One has been enacted from the very beginning of human life … The other story began to be enacted here some ten thousand years ago by the founders of your culture and is apparently about to end in catastrophe."[42]

Ishmael taught me to look at "common sense beliefs" I had never thought to question—the way a fish doesn't question the water it swims in. *Ishmael* quickly changed my perspective of our society, and left me perplexed that I had never noticed its red flags before.

Keeping the garden in my mind pruned and beautiful was hard while reading this book. Not only did it put into question my beliefs for a second time, but it put into question *the*

---

42   Quinn, Daniel. 1992. Ishmael.

whole of modern human's existence. I will talk more about *Ishmael's* teachings in later chapters.

Ishmael was absolutely amazing and enlightening. At the same time though, the light was now shining on things that were beyond my control—bigger egoic monsters and sneakier shadows, alive and thriving.

The truth that *Ishmael* exposed me to left me absolutely terrified, and there were nights I cried myself to sleep while reading this book. The new information made me feel helpless at times, but I was determined to use my new knowledge to make a positive change—one that could hopefully shift the direction of every person on the planet.

My intensity and sense of urgency to make a radical change only heightened after I worked a summer in South Africa. I was brought face-to-face with the implications of the problems I, as an American consumer, was largely ignorant to. The overarching lack of awareness around dire problems like climate change, consumption of resources, animal poaching, and mass extinction made me feel hopeless.

Trying to explain why I thought things should change was hard to do, especially in the face of innocent ignorance. I could never accurately put together a quick explanation why I held the perspective I did—there was too much to it.

It felt like I needed my own book just to explain myself.

***

Shortly thereafter, now in my senior year of college, I was recommended yet another book by *two* people close to me—a sure sign from the Magic that this book was of importance to my life.

OUTWITTING THE DEVIL BY NAPOLEON HILL

Hill was an American self-help author whose book *Think and Grow Rich* became one of the top ten best-selling self-help books of all time. *Outwitting the Devil* was written in 1938, but Hill didn't publish until both he and his wife were dead—likely avoiding controversy, as the book is ahead of its time. It finally published in 2011.

Hill taught readers how to outwit "the Devil," which he deemed purely mind-made—only the negative thoughts running rampant in your mind, mostly comprised of fear. He pointed out ways in which "the Devil" goes about his tasks, cleverly masked and working invisibly within society.

It was eerily reminiscent of what *Ishmael* had taught me about our current culture.

Hill also determined his own laws of success and explained how to use them. He taught how he discovered his "other self," or his intuition, and how that faint, positive voice in his head guided him on this very book journey.

Though he went through periods of negativity, fear, and depression while writing the book, he used it all as a lesson to connect with his deeper self. His intuition was the voice that led him down a foggy, dim-lit road to success. He had to go out on an invisible limb and trust himself to write this book based on the quiet guidance in his head.

With little to no plan, he started to believe in his own success, and listened to his intuition step-by-step. And it worked! He later became *one of the most famous self-help authors ever to live.*

His teachings were but a mash-up of all the previous books I had read. He said anyone can make their lives into anything they want it to be, and that they can receive help:

> "Recognize that your brain is a receiving set that can be attuned to receive communications from the universal store-house of Infinite Intelligence, to help you transmute your desires into their physical equivalent."[43]

---

43 Hill, Napoleon, Sharon L Lechter, Mark Victor Hansen, and Michael Bernard Beckwith. 2011. Outwitting The Devil.

What he deemed Infinite Intelligence I had been calling "Magic." I knew that we spoke of the same thing, and that his words were true—especially in regard to my past reading history. He helped me understand just how to accomplish my goal of having a big impact.

This was the final book that inspired me to move to action. Now, I felt compelled to write a book like Napoleon Hill's—a modern approach to the philosophy he completed. And I knew, as Hill taught me, that all I needed to do was follow my own inner voice in order to make my dream come to life.

That little voice would connect me to the Magic—that I had been trailing for so many years. I knew it would then guide me to the experiences needed for me to complete a real book, at only twenty-two years old. I could feel in my soul how important all of this surprising information was, and that it could be used on behalf of *all* life.

But I had a feeling, likely a nudge from my intuition, that if I were to write my own book I would surely be driven to my own point of helplessness before the book would be published—just as Mr. Hill had. It seems like no coincidence that my entire foundation came crashing down around me *for the second time* as soon as I began writing—reminiscent of Napoleon Hill's experiences.

During a time period of about three months, I:

- Got diagnosed with a heart condition
- Injured my knee and couldn't walk
- Got incredibly sick and stayed on bedrest
- Nearly got sent to a behavioral hospital
- Missed seven weeks of school, just before finals and graduation
- Only left my apartment for physical therapy and counseling twice a week
- Went through a breakup
- Lost fifteen pounds
- Finished school from bed and, luckily, graduated
- Moved back to Utah
- Found a hole in my heart
- Got diagnosed with autoimmune and connective tissue disorder
- Discovered a gene mutation pre-disposing me to thousands of chronic diseases

Through it all, I continued to write a book about how to make Magic—despite the gnawing of imposter syndrome. I trusted myself and where life was taking me, though it sure as hell did not feel Magical at this point in time.

It was my chance to finally apply all that I had learned to see if it would work for myself. I had to prove to life, just like Hill, that I, too, could be brave enough to listen to my intuition. After all, he said his struggles happened to give him the confidence he needed to use his theories on himself in real life.

Even Eckhart Tolle said, "Life will give you whatever experience is most helpful for the evolution of your consciousness."[44] The health scare led me to new information on keeping the body and mind healthy, which I use in this book, so I now understand why those challenges faced me.

My hope is that you can use what I've learned to help yourself work some Magic in your own life.

***

Now that you understand the pathway of books I took that led me down the rabbit hole, you know the basis of the life-changing things that I learned from reading the stories of others:

- Thoughts can be Magic
- We live in a spiritual, seemingly Magical reality, and science *actually* agrees
- Bodies are run by Magic

---

44 Tolle, Eckhart. 2005. A New Earth. London: Penguin.

- We can use Magic by connecting to our intuition
- Magic is always helping and guiding us

Books contain Magic unique to each person. To begin your own Magical book journey, I suggest starting with an intention of what you're looking for, what you're wanting to learn, or where you need guidance. You can use that to guide you to a certain genre.

Begin noticing what books or authors within that genre catch your attention. Maybe read a few pages and see how you feel. If your insides are jumping around with excitement, you can bet you've stumbled upon your own book Magic.

PART II:

In this section you will be introduced to the idea of humans as authors and life as your book. You will learn more about seemingly invisible patterns and structures at work in the world today, the ways that they bring harm, as well as how they've stayed in place for so long. It explains what could happen if we abandoned the current storylines and replaced them with a happier, more loving plot. Lastly, I share with you the four Magical guidelines that have shaped the way I live my life as an empowered author of my own life story.

CHAPTER 4:

LIFE AS A STORY

——

"Whatever man believes to be true has a way of becoming true."

—NAPOLEON HILL[45]

One of the most Magical things about life is that we have the chance to create our own, dreamy life story.

We might think of ourselves as the main characters of our story, hoping to get to the storyline we most desire. In your individual story, the world revolves around you, and you experience the world as only you can.

---

45 Hill, Napoleon, Sharon L Lechter, Mark Victor Hansen, and Michael Bernard Beckwith. 2011. Outwitting The Devil.

You get to act according to your unique desires, opinions, and situations, with each choice you make leading you to a different version of how your story continues. The choices made in *your* story goes on to affect the way *other peoples' stories* continue as well.

After reading *A New Earth*, however, I realized that I am *not* simply the main character of my story, with my thoughts acting as the narrator. More accurately, I am the powerful *author* of my story, creating each narration, experience, and character—*including* the main character.

When asked who you are, you may come up with:

- A name
- A backstory
- Your job title
- Where you live
- How you grew up

You will look to your perceptual foundation and pyramid of met or unmet human needs to define you. These are great stories, identifiers, or labels *for the main character*—but these are not *you*.

In regard to the conceptualized main character, Tolle said, "This is the ego. This illusory sense of self is what Albert

Einstein, who had deep insights not only into the reality of space and time but also into human nature, referred to as an 'optical illusion of consciousness.'"[46]

You are not, in fact, the main character, but the author of the main character's story.

Jim Carrey once said, "I realized that I could lose myself in a character. I could live in a character ... And the shift was, 'Wait a second. If I can put Jim Carey aside for four months, who is Jim Carrey? ... I now know that he does not really exist. He's ideas ...'"[47]

Your main character also consists of ideas. Whereas, the author—who you truly are—is limitless and can create its main character and life story to be absolutely anything it desires.

The author is the creative observer in the background of all of your thought's narrations. The author consists of pure consciousness—of which everything else in existence is made of as well.

---

46   Tolle, Eckhart. 2005. A New Earth. London: Penguin.
47   Sturm, Rudiger. 2019. "Jim Carrey | The Talks." The Talks.

Max Planck, the founder of quantum mechanics, said, "As a man who has devoted his whole life to the most clear headed science, to the study of matter, I can tell you as a result of my research about the atoms this much: *There is no matter as such!*"[48]

He stated, "I regard consciousness as fundamental. I regard matter as derivative from consciousness. We cannot get behind consciousness. Everything that we talk about, everything that we regard as existing, postulates consciousness."[49]

Plank pointed to the fact that physical matter we see and experience is all a *result* of consciousness. Therefore, there must be a universal consciousness *thinking all things into existence*. Your inner essence is a part of this universal "mind."

That means that *you can also think things into existence.* This is science! *You are an author.* You and the overarching universal consciousness are co-authors. Together, you can make Magic.

Dr. Joe Dispenza, neuroscientist and author of *Becoming Supernatural,* says, "Tuning into the energy of your future

---

48 Dossey, Larry. 2016. "Pseudoscience Versus Science." Physics Today
49 Ibid.

and intentionally observing that potential … causes infinite fields of energy to collapse into particles, called a quantum event, and that becomes an experience that can manifest in your physical, three-dimensional world."[50]

However, most of us are unaware of this Magical ability of creation by thought, because we are identifying with what our inner narrator tells us instead. We too easily box ourselves in. But you have actually been more of the victim than the perpetrator.

Your mind has tricked you. It has repeated:

- Stories
- Old, conditioned thoughts and programming
- Comments from people who have hurt you
- Images from your past
- Fears about your future

Your mind has reaffirmed thoughts to you so often that they hardened into your being and so have become a part of "you" and your life story. It has tried to destine you to a future filled with the same repeated thoughts, fears, and patterns you experience now.

---

50   Dispenza, Joe. 2017. "Becoming Supernatural." Google Books.

Your thought's narrations can convince you of a false reality. Your mind may repeat things to you so frequently that you might believe they are true and that that voice is your own.

We tend to tune out reality for this false narration instead of getting in touch with our inner space and being present within the Now. Rarely do we genuinely take in our surroundings during the present moment we are actually living.

That is OK, it is not your fault. You likely did not realize this taking place, just as I didn't realize it before I read *A New Earth*. But with this new awareness, you *can* change your story.

You are not your thoughts. You are the awareness that has the ability to perceive and interact with the world around you in whichever way it pleases—*you are the author.*

You are the conscious presence that allows thought to arise, that loves and laughs, and that recognizes beauty. You are the intelligence that breathes, blinks and heals cuts and bruises without even having to think about it.

You are complete Magic. And once more deeply in touch with this Magic, which I am guiding you toward throughout this book, you will discover ways to become the author of your own, dreamy life story.

Personally, one of my outlandish dreams was to write a book. It seemed close to impossible, but I stood in my rightful place as the author of my story, and began to tell people I was writing a book. I knew that if I said it would happen, it would eventually happen.

I decided to think my own book into existence.

As an author, I instructed the main character of my story to take the baby steps needed to get closer to that dream. Along the way, because I was determined to achieve my goal and was taking slow but consistent steps toward my dream, Magic stepped in.

The opportunity to write a book found me, at the age of only twenty-two. I never would've believed just a year ago that I would be in the position I am now. Yet, I realize that I am the one who empowered myself to create this as a part of my story.

That same kind of Magic can happen for you, too, once you step into your own power as the author of your life.

***

The collective humanity tries to author its story as well, at times unsuccessfully, as unified desires are harder to pinpoint and enact on such a large scale. That requires a global consciousness.

In the global story of humanity, each collective choice we make will still lead us to a different version of how this story continues. "Quantum science suggests the existence of many possible futures for each moment of our lives. Each future lies in a state of rest until it is awakened by choices made in the present," according to Gregg Braden, author of *The Science of Self-Empowerment*.[51]

Our story *now* affects the way future generations of peoples' stories will be shaped, like a ripple effect. Will we give future generations a fighting chance, or we leave them to handle the outcomes of our current problems?

When asked who humans are as a collective, many of us may reply that we are the masters of the world, and the smartest, most evolved beings on the planet. Many of us probably believe we are the smartest—if not the only—beings in the whole universe. Everything is at our fingertips, and we have the idea that things will always be this way.

Others may respond that we are greedy and destructive as a species. I'm sure some think that we are born flawed and

---

51   Braden, Gregg. 2000. "The Isaiah Effect." Google Books.

will only continue to inflict pain and suffering on ourselves and others, as has been the case for so long.

However, beneath the surface, the truth is that we are all exactly the same: Human, made of stardust, water, sunlight and elements. Most of us seem to be unaware of this truth, more concerned with judgment and division based on superficiality such as appearance.

At this current point in our narrative, we live in an age of technology and information. We actually exist in a near-constant state of macro-consciousness, given access to the internet.

Though our world still revolves around us individually, we are now being exposed to the worlds of others through:

- Photos
- Tweets
- Memes
- Shared or liked posts
- The news
- YouTube videos

Any question you ever ask can be answered in less than a second with a simple Google search. As a result, our consciousness of other life on this planet is expanding quickly.

In this time of technology, information and knowledge should be something that all individuals seek in order to better their own life story as well as the story of our generation—for the story of our generation will invariably affect those to come for the rest of time.

Buddha once said, "Three things cannot long be hidden: The sun, the moon, and the truth."[52] Once truthful information has been discovered, it is crucially important to not hide it away in fear, but to embrace it.

Truth can be a double-edged sword. We say we want the truth, but often times it is still difficult to accept, so we fear it. We will go so far as to deny the truth even as it looks us dead in the face.

I have definitely been slapped by the truth many times as I've gone seeking it. Most of the information that has hurt me are things that proved me wrong, or things I would never consider moral. I was hurt by learning of things that I never knew happened, things that went on right under my nose, or by learning I had been misinformed by people I trusted.

Information has led me, time and time again, to things that I definitely would have felt better not knowing … at least

---

52 "Buddha On Truth." 2019. Spiritualityhealth.Com.

initially. It can be painful to bear the burden of admitting we are wrong, or having to change our rigid thoughts, beliefs, or behavior. Sometimes ignorance to the truth can be bliss.

But in this age of information, blissful ignorance is something that should not continue, however joyful it may be. That bliss is a total illusion, unable to be seen through by most—for ignorance is unseen by the ignorant.

The same information that hurt or scared me, as was the norm while reading *Ishmael,* is the same honest truth I feel is of utmost importance for not just me, but for every breathing human to know.

I will dedicate the next chapter to this information, because nothing can be learned from if it is not looked at first, no matter how scary or controversial it may seem.

What may initially come off as shocking soon becomes bearable, and then acceptable. Once the new information is accepted, you get to act accordingly with a new, heightened level of awareness. You can then consciously work to change things around if you so please, because you now know that something you don't like actually *exists.*

Even being slapped by the truth is much better than never knowing. Knowledge is power. Wisdom is the quality of discernment and decisions made on behalf of that power.

It is our choice now to become collectively wise.

***

We all are a part of the collective storyline of the Earth—a living, breathing being that is in constant cycles of transformation, death, and rebirth. It is amazing that we all get to take part in the creation of that storyline. Not one of our voices should be more or less important than the next.

The story we are enacting at this moment has a few possible endings. These endings may be happening soon, given the mass destruction humans have caused and continue to cause. A few possible causes being discussed are:

- Climate change
- A world war
- Nuclear destruction
- Lack of/destruction/over-consumption of resources
- Overtaking of artificial intelligence

There are crucial decisions that need to be made about how the human race continues from here, which require the perspective of *all* who will be affected. With the help of modern technology, we can merge our personal stories into collective stories with people across the world. I think we need to—regardless of culture, religion, race, or gender.

A unified vision is important.

For *the first time in human history*, we have an opportunity for the collective decision of how our global story continues. This is the first time in our history that we can learn the previous chapters of our own and of others' history, with the click of a few buttons.

We have the opportunity to set the stage for the next chapters of this story we call life on Earth. Consciously, we can become the collective authors of a more positive future for everyone.

We have a glaring opportunity to become unified by knowledge, wisdom, peace, love, and compassion. We are all human, wishing for the happiness and well-being of ourselves, others, and this planet. Each and every last one of us deserves it.

Right now, we have the choice to put our egos aside and make that happen. How our story will continue from here— or if it will continue at all—needs to be determined as soon as possible.

We must understand that our choices now affect all the other life on the planet, including animals, plants, even your grandchildren, and will for the rest of time.

Now is the time for humans to collectively set goals bigger and better than we can imagine possible. Gordon in the *Secret Nature of Matter* said, "Some things may only seem impossible because no one has tried them. And usually no one has tried them because everyone believes they are impossible. It's a self-perpetuating cycle."[53]

I am telling you that it is *OK* to dream up and enact the seemingly impossible. It only takes one person to break that cycle.

If we become aware of the problems we face and take action toward bettering things, Magic has a chance to step in to help us heal the planet. If we set goals, regardless of how unattainable they may seem to us now, and work slowly but surely toward achieving them, we will be able to do more than even imagined.

Baby steps is all it takes. But we must begin to write in dreams as collective authors before it is too late. The possible endings

---

53   Gordon, Richard. 2017. Secret Nature Of Matter.

that we are being faced with at this point in time affect not just humans—they wipe out most of the life on the planet.

Before writing in a new storyline, we must ask ourselves:

- *How did things come to be this way, anyways?*
- *What story carried us all here?*
- *How the hell did this happen?*

CHAPTER 5:

THE RUNNING
STORYLINES

___

"That's the premise of your story: The world was made for man."
—DANIEL QUINN[54]

The current global storyline is the course of human action
that is alive and active today—the narrative we are writing
of our past, our present, and our foreseeable plans for our
future. It is probable that it is, unknowingly, *part of the reason
you are reading this book.*

---

54 Quinn, Daniel. 1992. Ishmael.

There are many factors that contribute to the current yet out-dated human storyline, including:

- Genetics
- Family tradition
- Trauma
- Imbalance
- School
- Religion
- Capitalism
- Consumerism
- Technological improvements

In *Outwitting the Devil*, the Devil confesses, " … my hell is here on earth and not in the world that comes after death … drifters supply all the fire I use in my hell."[55] Drifters are the people living like zombies, sleepwalking through their days. They are the people moving numbly through life with no passion, aim, or purpose—those who are under the spell of the current storyline.

Napoleon Hill knew that "man has not yet fully awakened to the realization of his potential power."[56] Our culture also has not yet learned to use our power in the service of much,

---

55 Hill, Napoleon, Sharon L Lechter, Mark Victor Hansen, and Michael Bernard Beckwith. 2011. Outwitting The Devil.
56 Ibid.

other than madness. In Daniel Quinn's novel *Ishmael*, Ishmael asks, "Among the people of your culture, which want to destroy the world?"[57]

My answer, along with yours I'm sure, is that *no one wants* to destroy the world. Ishmael continues, "And yet you do destroy it, each of you. Each of you contributes daily to the destruction of the world ... You're captives of a civilizational system that more or less compels you to go on destroying the world in order to live."[58]

"I'm telling you this," Ishmael says, "because the people of your culture are captives of a story ... It's like the humming of a distant motor that never stops; it becomes a sound that's no longer heard at all."[59] We are all captives of a story that says this world was made for us.

As I learned from *Ishmael*, the lot of us have grown up thinking the divine intentions for the world we live in was to evolve up until the birth of man, and *that was the entire point*. We literally think the *entire point* of this world was to be *created for humans*—for us to conquer and rule it. We truly believe the world is here to *serve us*.

---

57 Quinn, Daniel. 1992. Ishmael.
58 Ibid.
59 Ibid.

In Ishmael's words, "Once you learn to discern the ... humming in the background ... you'll never stop being conscious of it. Wherever you go for the rest of your life, you'll be tempted to say to the people around you, 'How can you listen to this stuff and not recognize it for what it is?' And if you do this, people will look at you oddly and wonder what the devil you're talking about."[60]

The humming in the background is the many ways people's beliefs and subsequent actions go on destroying the world every day. Many do not realize that their unquestioned actions are indeed contributing to the death and destruction of other environments, people, and animals. Many are unaware that our consumption of our planet is, in fact, detrimental to us in the long run.

We see and hear signs of our own demise every day, with special action being taken by *children* such as environmental activist and sixteen year old Greta Thunberg—though a lot of us brush it off either in indifference, disbelief or helplessness. I know now what it is like to be that person—to want to scream, "*CAN'T YOU SEE IT?*" in the face of destructive narratives, like man ruling the world—but to be looked at oddly, as if I am acting delusional.

---

60 Ibid.

You may not believe me, but the science behind our earth's rapid devastation is no longer a matter of belief. And as Ishmael states, "Belief is not required. Once you know this story, you'll hear it everywhere in your culture, and you'll be astonished that the people around you don't hear it as well but merely take it in … "[61]

My hope is that enough of us—billions of us, at least—will recognize the parts of this story that we are captives of in order to become conscious of it and so change the narrative. We must learn of our story of captivity in order to set goals that will carry us out of it.

The future of all life on this planet depends on it.

***

THE STORY HOLDING US CAPTIVE

The world was made for man, so we treat the world however we damn well please.

Put simply, humans are unbothered by constant reproduction and expansion—in fact, we admire it. As a result, we are overpopulating and consuming this planet to the point of

---

61   Ibid.

destruction and extinction. Here's a visual of human population growth, by billions, to help you understand:

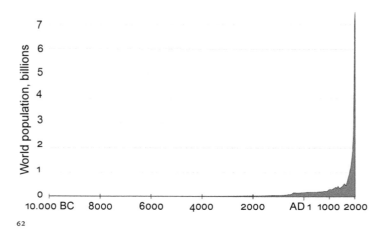

62

The earliest members of the "homo" genus evolved nearly 3
million years ago[63], and they lived peacefully on this planet
as hunter-gatherers, co-existing with plants, animals, and
their environment. These are the humans we tend to deem
"primitive" or "animalistic." Ishmael pointed out that we
assume "150,000 generations of humans could live and go
down to death with nothing in their heads or lives worth
knowing."[64]

62 "Human Overpopulation." 2019. En.Wikipedia.Org.
63 "'First Human' Discovered In Ethiopia." 2019. BBC News.
64 Quinn, Daniel. 1992. Ishmael.

For that stretch of time, humans existed on this planet just as animals did—according to the cycles of nature and the laws of food competition. Though we were not preyed on, other animals could still compete with us for food sources. The food web was balanced, and all existed according to nature's law.

About 10,000 years ago in the Fertile Crescent (coinciding with the birth of Adam and Eve—though we now know they were *not* the first humans on earth) somebody decided they were sick of living constantly on the move, hunting for food. That person thought humans should not be at the whim of nature, but should instead be able to control how they eat and live, resting in one place as long as they choose.

They were decidedly above nature, refusing to live any longer as "animals." They thought they should be able to sustain their own lives regardless of nature's regulated cycles and delicate balance of life. This monumental event (coinciding with Adam's expulsion from the Garden of Eden) was the birth of food production—the beginnings of the agricultural revolution.

We deem this to be one of the best technological advancements in history... But is that true?

The beginning of agriculture was the distinct point in time that we disconnected ourselves from nature—from Magic. This marked the rise of the delusional human ego, thriving on separation, which now casts its shadow all over the world. Humans started to believe that we, with our intellect, knew better than the wisdom of the Gods, better than the nature around us.

So we sought to become a more "civilized" species.

When in line with nature's laws, we killed only what we needed to survive. Now, we resorted to hoarding mass food supply for the future, rather than eating as we needed. The business of agriculture went on as an act of control and manipulation.

We expanded to killing *any* competition that stood in the way of resources that we thought clearly *belonged to us*. We didn't kill just for survival, we killed for control—to keep conditions optimal for *our* growth and expansion. Now, in the present, we also kill anything we think has any slight benefit to us.

We have deemed ourselves better than *the rest of the planet*, as well as exempted ourselves from the earth's natural laws, which keep populations, food supply, and the whole delicate food-chain at equilibrium.

As our food supply grows, so does our population, despite the fact that there are still people starving. Peter Farb, an anthropologist, ecologist, and biologist, said, "Intensification of production to feed an increased population leads to a still greater increase in population."[65]

Now, amid technological improvements in agriculture and health, we have quickly exploded into a population of 7.7 billion people.[66] "The world population today is 1,860-times the size of what it was 12 millennia ago when the world population was around 4 million—half of the current population of London," according to Max Roser, an economist at Oxford and founder of *Our World in Data*.[67]

Ishmael points out to us humans, " ... you're so accustomed to the sudden utterly fantastic rise of your population beginning ten thousand years ago that it no longer *seems* utterly fantastic to you. On the contrary, it seems completely unremarkable ... Yet it's precisely this surge that has made you the enemy of all life on this planet."[68]

---

65 Ibid.
66 "World Population Clock: 7.7 Billion People (2019) – Worldometers." 2019. Worldometers.Info.
67 Roser, Max, Hannah Ritchie, and Esteban Ortiz-Ospina. 2019. "World Population Growth." Our World In Data.
68 Quinn, Daniel. 1992. Ishmael.

Yet, we go on with the cultural storyline of growing up, making money, and having a family. The idea of population control is considered cruel, and free birth control is highly debated. However, reigning in our population's growth is one of the only options we have for giving this planet a fighting chance, according to Ishmael.

"At one billion, I suspect you could have lived here for millions of years, perhaps for the life of this planet," Ishmael says. "But driven by the habit of thought that insists that you must increase food production every year in order to feed your growing population, you failed (and continue to fail) to see that it is this very habit of thought that has driven your populations precipitous and catastrophic growth."[69]

This modern human storyline, based on the premise that this world was made for us, is not working any longer. By losing our connection with nature, we have also lost our closest connection to Magic. Today's global storyline has become a false and dangerous narrative—resulting in a world for only the white man to thrive in.

We must change the direction of our thoughts and beliefs on a macro-scale in order to escape captivity and change the outcome of this story.

---

69 Ibid.

Ishmael finishes, "… the dire predictions I've made to you about the future are less dire than the reality that faces us … Biologists worldwide are by now agreed that we are already in the midst of a Sixth Extinction as dire as the Fifth, this one precipitated entirely by a single species, *yours*."[70]

***

CONTRIBUTING STORIES

This anthropogenic culture of humans dominating and holding life captive, now being deemed the Anthropocene, is all a lot of us have ever known. It is the shadow that hides in plain sight, the incessant humming we've grown accustomed to and no longer notice.

A shadow only stays a shadow, however, until the light of awareness shines on it. Then, it becomes a making of our own energy and creation. From there, we can consciously choose to stop prolonging the life of the shadow and its destructive narrative altogether.

What does this collective shadow look like right now, in the year 2019?

---

70   Ibid.

In *Outwitting the Devil*, the Devil made a confession: "Parents, schoolteachers, religious instructors and many other adults unknowingly serve my purpose by helping me to destroy in children the habit of thinking for themselves. They go about their work in various ways, never suspecting what they are doing to the minds of children or the real cause of children's mistakes."

CULTURAL TRADITION

During a seven-week internship in South Africa where I thought I would be taking photos of wild animals, I actually helped the anti-poaching movement alongside Dr. William Fowlds, wildlife veterinarian. He contributed to the effort of saving rhinos by chain-sawing rhinoceros' horns off of their faces. A horn is worth more money on the black market than gold or cocaine.

There are only a few ways at the moment to try and save rhinos from people who will murder them to sell their horn. Removing the horn safely with trained veterinarians is one of the most efficient, for now.

Unfortunately, the horn is also a rhino's method of self-defense, as their sweet, little eyes can't see predators from a distance. Knowing full well that these animals would have little to nothing to defend themselves in the wild, we went ahead and took their magnificence from them anyway, in the best attempt we had to ward off fellow humans.

Either way, the rhino loses.

While helping dehorn my first rhino, I got to feel its rough skin and the soft patches behind its ears. We even made it into the newspaper, under the impression that we had saved a life of a dying species. A week later, regardless of the horn's absence, that same rhino was killed.

To be so close with a majestic, God-like animal, and do all you can to prolong its life, then get the news of its murder … it broke my heart.

Each death takes a toll on the wildlife veterinarians who risk their lives every day to save these poor animals. But in this specific rhino's case, it took an even larger toll on its orphaned baby, who was forced to watch its mother suffer and die.

"These days the main threat to the surviving rhinos comes from the illegal rhino horn trade between Africa and Asia. Certain buyers in Vietnam and China—the largest and second-largest black market destinations respectively—covet rhino horn products for different reasons. Some purchase horn chunks or powder for traditional medicinal purposes, to ingest or to give others as an impressive gift," according to the Scientific American.[71]

In reality, a rhino horn is essentially a giant fingernail. Really, it's made of keratin, and it holds zero health benefits whatsoever. Still, people are buying it because of unquestioned collective belief in its value, and so rhinos go on being murdered to the point of near-extinction.

While face-to-face with the tragedy of it all, I wondered:

- *Should I brush this off as simply supply and demand?*
- *Should I continue on with life as normal, because maybe someone somewhere will come up with a fix to poaching?*
- *Should I not think twice about this, because crushed rhino horn is an important part of somebody's culture or storyline?*

Rhino poaching is but one of the many troubling problems currently looming over us. Luckily, this particular shadow is starting to become illuminated. However, inaccurate human beliefs are still a reason that innocent animals are being decimated.

---

71 Hsu, Jeremy. 2019. "The Hard Truth About The Rhino Horn "Aphrodisiac" Market." Scientific American.

These types of unquestioned cultural narratives, held by numerous amounts of people, are a part of the collective shadow. Dangerous beliefs and traditions of all kinds are still in full swing in many parts of the world. We *must* begin to look critically at cultural tradition and its effect on people and our world.

FAMILY TRADITION

The Devil in *Outwitting the Devil* admits that he will "cause the parents to teach their children to believe as the parents do in connection with religion, politics, marriage, and other important subjects." By using this tactic, the Devil "can easily perpetuate control."[72]

Most parents teach their kids the same things *they* were taught when *they* were children. A lot of parents wish for their children to conform to their own wants and needs. Some parents even attempt to live out their own dreams through their children.

Napoleon Hill explained, "Science has established irrefutable evidence that people are what they are because of heredity and environment. They bring over with them at birth ... the physical qualities of all their numberless ancestors ... from

---

72 Hill, Napoleon, Sharon L Lechter, Mark Victor Hansen, and Michael Bernard Beckwith. 2011. Outwitting The Devil.

there on they shape their own personalities as the result of the environmental influences to which they are subjected."[73]

Our parents have also been conditioned to believe, think, feel, and act certain ways by their own parents, who were likely taught the same by *their* parents. It is a generational cycle that continues endlessly until one person becomes aware of it, and so steps out of it.

There are many family traditions or patterns running that may be harmful to children—kids may feel trapped in a certain lifestyle, or forced to follow a path they don't connect with. I know many who feel the need to continue on in a family business even though they hate it, or keep dating people they don't truly love, because they think it is what their parents want.

Tradition can be stifling. It is expected to be respected and stood by, but times change. Parenting should shift with the times.

Chapter one explained how children's brains are extremely impressionable and largely shaped by the age of five. Children up to that age learn how to fulfill their pyramid of needs by imitation.

---

73   Ibid.

"Imitation becomes a fixed habit. Naturally the child imitates, first of all, its parents! Then it begins to imitate its other relatives and daily associates ... the child picks up fear through the habit of imitation and stores it away as a part of its subconscious stock of beliefs," according to Napoleon Hill.[74]

One must question family teachings and traditions. One should become aware of how their personal family narratives affect:

- Their own mental, emotional, spiritual, and physical well-being
- The well-being of one's children
- Their opinions and views about relationships, religion, politics, etc.
- The way one copes with stress or problems
- The way one relates to other people
- How one acts within the world

Again, a negative family narrative will be perpetually re-cycled through the family line until one person becomes aware of it and changes it.

---

74   Ibid.

The Devil in *Outwitting the Devil* confessed, "I especially need the help of those who give children their religious instruction, because it is here that I break down independent thought … by confusing their minds with unprovable ideas concerning a world of which they know nothing. It is here also that I plant in the minds of children the greatest of all the fears—the fear of hell!"[75]

In Christianity, there is a belief that the world will one day be destroyed and that only those who acted in alignment with God will be saved. I guess you could say the Bible predicts the end of the world. I guess you could also say, according to scientific evidence, that the Bible-prophesied end of the world may actually be happening *now*.

What many evangelical religious groups may fail to grasp is the actual result of the story they fully intend to spread to the hastily growing population of this Earth: the anticipation of our own destruction.

Many people see and hear the signs of our destruction, yet feel no burning need to do anything about it because of the belief that a higher, external power will come take care of things when we mess it up too bad. Since the best of Christ's

---

75   Ibid.

followers are already taken care of, it doesn't matter how we treat the Earth we live on.

But these stories also rely on the idea of God passing judgement on us, the opposite of unconditional love. If we were born of a God who loves us, why would he strike us down to hell for not obeying well enough? If I put this in the context of my actual father and I, that sounds a bit like manipulation to me, possibly emotional abuse.

Not a single one of us is perfect. So then, who would actually be making it to this heaven they speak of in books like the Bible?

I'm not saying religious books are wrong, or bad. All I am saying is that maybe we could put collective thought into the manifestation of a happier, more peaceful ending—one that doesn't fantasize the destruction of the only inhabitable planet we know of.

The point is, we have lived our lives in accordance with these stories for so long that we have forgotten we have the ability to write our own.

We have unconsciously been bringing about our own destruction, because many have put intense collective belief into the idea that the world ending is a marvelous, divine thing. We have also largely given up any power we have over our own fate for an external source to do our bidding.

Why should we put our own power and belief into an external religious idea, if we don't know whether it's entirely truthful?

I like to think of the game Telephone, where one person whispers a sentence to the next person, and it carries all the way down the row of people until the last person says aloud the message they received. The game is fun because the message gets confused and jumbled and misinterpreted, then by the end it's a completely different sentence. How funny!

The first of the Bible stories were passed down orally, as writing was first invented only 5,000 years ago.[76] Assuming Bible stories began to be told 10,000 years ago (the time Adam and Eve were "born"), for 5,000 years these stories were passed along orally.

How are we to trust that these Bible stories are true? Would they not be comparable to playing a game of telephone for 5,000 years?

Religious storylines can be harmful in multiple ways. It sets restrictive rules and lifestyles for people to live. When people

---

76   "Ancient History". 2019. En.M.Wikipedia.Org.

"mess up," they feel the heat of God looking down on them, or the fear of the Devil's temptation. It takes the most powerful force in the world and labels it with a human gender, leaving women feeling inferior.

Religion then becomes a game of conformity, and spiritual caging. Religious storylines bleed into all other areas of our lives, including relationships, experiences, even politics and legislation.

"The only thing of enduring value to any human being is a working knowledge of his own mind. The churches do not permit a person to inquire into the possibilities of his own mind, and the schools do not recognize that such a thing as a mind exists," explained Hill.[77]

We must question the rules of religions we have followed obediently, and the way that they affect other areas of life, including but not limited to:

- Mental, emotional and spiritual wellbeing
- Political systems
- The economy
- The relation of ourselves to people, the planet, and other life forms

77 Hill, Napoleon, Sharon L Lechter, Mark Victor Hansen, and Michael Bernard Beckwith. 2011. Outwitting The Devil.

- Marriage and family life
- Human rights and freedoms

SCHOOL AND HISTORICAL TRADITION

The school system is still running its own storyline as well, teaching students *what* to think rather than *how* to think.

Napoleon Hill said, "School children are not taught to develop and use their own minds, but to adopt and use the thoughts of others … there is no definite plan or purpose behind any of the school curricula! Children are sent to school to make credits and to learn how to memorize, not to learn what they want of life."[78]

Within school there is a further, unspoken, reinforcement for students to simply trust their superiors. Students are taught to respect authority and be obedient. There is fear around asking questions, and an unspoken belief that if someone asks a question they are dumb for not understanding.

Instead of going to school to learn, one goes to school with fear of not knowing enough. Students of all ages are instilled with fear of underperforming and not getting that "A" grade. Students compare themselves to others who perform better,

---

78 Ibid.

and try to turn in work in-line with the teachers specifications—leaving little room for creativity or expression.

Students must usually:

- Be silent
- Raise their hands
- Not speak out of turn
- Write papers according to teachers' guidelines
- Ask for passes to use the bathroom
- Act according to the bell system

The school experience becomes robotic and does not teach students how to use their own minds effectively.

As I mentioned earlier, the invention of writing occurred only around 5,000 years ago. Until that time there was absolutely no first-hand recorded history. Yet, our history books often go unquestioned.

For example, "For 10 years, students in Texas have used a history textbook that says not all slaves were unhappy." The textbook stated, "Many may not have even been terribly unhappy with their lot, for they knew no other."[79]

---

79 Annabelle Timsit, Annalisa Merelli. 2019. "For 10 Years, Students In Texas Have Used A Textbook That Says Not All Slaves Were Unhappy." Quartz.

Most do not take into account the fact that history is written by people who contain bias, judgement, pride, and the spectrum of emotions. Twenty people can witness a fight and in the end, there will be twenty different versions of the same one fight.

But history is written by the living and the winning... So what happens to the history of the dead man, or animal? What happens to the history of the being who no longer has a voice to be heard?

If you take into account the world's deadly past, filled with rape, violence, murders, and wars against our own kind, you must know that history is, indeed, written by the winners— the people still alive to tell the story. The winner may see nothing wrong with how they've done things because, look! They won!

And the winner's side of the story will be the one told proudly, as if worthy of firework shows. It does not matter that, say, American's, in pursuit of this country, may have inflicted:

- Warfare
- Violence
- Sexual abuse
- Torture
- Genocide

Those things do not matter, because this is now *our* land instead of *their* land. We won, and that is what will go down in history to be celebrated.

It will suffice to say that our current school systems are extremely outdated. We should be questioning the school tradition and searching for ways to upgrade or improve the system—for the sake of our children and our planet.

Question the history you've read in textbooks. Educate yourself and learn to discern truth from one-sided propaganda.

***

"If we are to change the world, the most powerful point of leverage is to change our fundamental core beliefs," stated Robert Gordon, boldly.[80]

It is time to start questioning the core beliefs of modern humans now, stemming from storylines that have been in place for hundreds of years of:

- Perceived separation from nature
- Belief that the world was made for only us

---

80 Gordon, Richard. 2017. Secret Nature Of Matter.

- Cultural tradition
- Family tradition
- Religious tradition
- Historical tradition
- School tradition

CHAPTER 6:

HOW STORIES STAY STRONG

___

"Our beliefs determine our attitudes. Our attitudes determine our thoughts and feelings, which in turn determine our choices and decisions."

—RICHARD GORDON[81]

Though books still somehow taught me the most, getting a formal education opened me up to a lot of information. It was studying advertising that led me to the conclusion that advertising is actually *complete bullshit*—nothing but convincing people that they need things they truly do

---

81   Ibid.

not. Advertising is using repetition and emotional manipulation to turn people into not much more than consumers—a destructive and pitiful way to define ourselves.

Eckhart Tolle mimicked my *own* thoughts, saying, "The
people in the advertising industry know very well that in
order to sell things that people don't really need, they must
convince them that those things will add something to how
they see themselves or are seen by others; in other words, add
something to their sense of self … in many cases you are not
buying a product but an 'identity enhancer.'"[82]

This is to say that advertising targets the ego, the false sense of
self, and makes you believe that buying things will make your
ego feel better. At the end of the day, both the ego as well as
the status gained from buying a product are illusory. Advertising and public relations put me in touch with the fact that
the things large corporations or institutions tell us are used
to keep us bound to living in a way that benefits *them—not us.*

Advertisements strategically create an "attachment to things,
obsession with things, which in turn creates our consumer
society and economic structures where the only measure of
progress is always *more* … The unchecked striving for more,
for endless growth, is a dysfunction and a disease. It is the

---

82   Tolle, Eckhart. 2005. A New Earth. London: Penguin.

same dysfunction the cancerous cell manifests, whose only goal is to multiply itself, unaware that it is bringing about its own destruction by destroying the organism of which it is a part," explained Tolle.[83]

In school I learned about *"effective frequency,"* an advertising term defined as "the theory that a consumer has to be exposed to an ad at least three times between two consecutive purchases to buy that product."[84] In other words, a message only need be repeated three times to make a person remember it, and even act on it.

✳✳✳

It was learning of the power of repetition in advertising that first led me to *really* question the repetitive narratives I had heard in the Mormon church. The decision to step away from my religion and educate myself on its history taught me a bit more than just repetition techniques; I learned about fear, control, and brainwashing.

For the first time in my life I was finding information about the "BITE method" of mind control, as researched and developed by Steven Hassan, an American mental health counselor.

---

83 Ibid.
84 "What Is Effective Frequency? Definition And Meaning." 2019. Businessdictionary.Com.

BITE METHOD OF MIND CONTROL:

BEHAVIOR CONTROL:

- Promote dependence and obedience
- Modify behavior with rewards and punishments
- Restrict or control sexuality, clothing, and hairstyle

INFORMATION CONTROL:

- Deliberately withhold and distort information
- Gaslight you to make you doubt your own memory
- Divide information into insider versus outsider doctrine

THOUGHT CONTROL:

- Instill black versus white, us versus them, good versus evil thinking
- Reject rational analysis, critical thinking, and doubt
- Use loaded language and clichés to stop complex thought

EMOTIONAL CONTROL:

- Label some emotions as evil, worldly, sinful, or wrong
- Promote feelings of guilt, shame, and unworthiness
- Shun you if you disobey or disbelieve[85]

I resonated with each of these bullet points, recognizing those behaviors from the LDS church. But I was shocked

---

85 "Steven Hassan's BITE Model – Freedom Of Mind Resource Center." 2019. Freedom Of Mind Resource Center.

that my old religion was so accurately defined by a list of "the specific methods that cults use to recruit and maintain control over people."[86]

Cults!

This taught me that controlling the information that people receive can distort their thought process. The person or people in control of information can use it to manipulate mass amounts of humans' thoughts using repetition, which in turn manipulates their emotions. By making people feel certain ways about certain things, their behavior is easily manipulated and controlled.

The BITE model's methods succeed at making people enact certain behaviors that they now believe are good, and avoiding behaviors that trigger thoughts that make them feel bad. This creates bias, judgement, hatred, fear, and division, among other things—all of which I had already noticed stemming from the LDS church and its culture. Distorted information had been taught to church members through:

- Weekly meetings
- Weekly activities
- Televised conferences

---

86 Ibid.

- Books
- Pamphlets
- Interviews
- Church magazines

I did not want to believe that the church I grew up in, the church that my friends and family are still a part of, could be a cult. Yet, there was no denying that the LDS church used these methods of mind control—and *well*. I wondered if we were all crazy to ever have gotten roped into such a thing? But I could only think of how easily guilt had kept me tied to the church's promises of salvation—with cooperation, of course.

***

Controlling people's behavior through the BITE model is said to be used in cults, but it can be just as easily used to propagate certain behaviors through today's mass media such as:

- Television
- Facebook
- Instagram
- Snapchat
- Twitter
- YouTube
- Advertisements on all of the above

Once an orchestrated narrative is repeated on one or more of the above three times, it sets into the brain like cement. Propaganda is at work nearly everywhere you look today.

When some or all of the techniques under the BITE method are used together, the result is that the mind becomes extremely obedient to group authority. It becomes entirely less able to think rationally, or to act independently. These experiences can, and are, used abusively to control and to manipulate people—and it can be as easy as, "Got milk?"

Most may not consciously realize why they think or act in certain ways. Many probably think it is of their own choosing, unconscious of the fact that they've been taking in controlled information. Some controllers may include, but are not limited to:

- Corporations
- News channels
- Politicians
- Religious institutions
- School systems

Even seemingly innocent bystanders such as your parents or family have also been roped in and thus add to the story's power simply by repeating what they have learned. Controlled information can easily become an unconscious belief, and many of those beliefs have likely been set in place since you were a child under the age of five.

It does not matter that you cannot consciously recognize these beliefs—they still influence you from a subconscious level. You will still act according to your emotions, not knowing they have been cleverly manipulated.

These imposed beliefs, no matter the source, make it harder for a person to think critically or independently. It may teach a distrust of outside sources. This is familiar within the LDS church, as well as on news channels that identify with a certain "side." This makes the audience rely heavily on internal information, which can then be further manipulated or controlled as the people in charge see fit.

The sources we rely on for information can become powerful, acting more like puppet masters rather than teachers.

***

IMPLICATIONS OF THESE STORIES

Though it may not be our fault that we've been unconsciously running false narratives, it is our duty now to become aware of the narratives in action and work to rewrite them. If not, we may face literal self-destruction—and that's not an over-exaggeration.

Today, as a result of distorted stories, we are faced with, among other things:

- Uneven distribution of wealth
- Uneven distribution of resources
- Imbalances of power
- War
- Violence
- Hatred
- Greed
- Constant production
- Rapid consumption
- Constant expansion

One of the most recent tragedies as a result of these imbalances was the fires ravaging the Amazon forest—our planet's *lungs*— and how they were started purposefully to clear land for cattle ranchers. Cattle ranching itself is responsible for as much as 80 percent of the ongoing deforestation of the Amazon rainforest.[87]

---

87   Zoë Schlanger, Daniel Wolfe. 2019. "Fires In The Amazon Rainforests Were Likely Intentional." Quartz.

Consumer culture, propagated by advertising, has repeatedly led to degradation of communities, homes, and ecosystems—both in America and in countries across the world. We likely don't know about the destruction our consumption has caused for people on the other side of the world due to globalization and outsourcing. We simply can't see it, and producers do not wish to tell us about it—they control what information they put out.

Yet, because of our constant consumption and destruction, "tens of species are vanishing from the face of the Earth every day ... 1,000-10,000 times faster than ... the normal extinction rate."[88] We cut down 3.5 billion to 7 billion trees each year,[89] despite the fact that trees provide us with the oxygen we breathe as well as inhale the carbon dioxide we are emitting in dangerous amounts.

We are destroying the planet we live on in order to maintain our fragile egos—our distorted sense of self.

Yet we, standing on this ball of dirt, *still* see ourselves as superior to every other existing thing on our planet—perhaps in our *universe*. Here we are, contemplating in reality the idea that, if we do happen to destroy this planet that provides us

---

88 "Wild Earth News & Facts By World Animal Foundation." 2019. Worldanimalfoundation.Com.
89 Ibid.

life, we can just move to a different one—and we are *literally scouting out Mars.*

And so we have, indeed, become like the cancer cell, inhabiting the planet until we use up or destroy everything it has to offer. Once this planet's human-caused death arises, we then plan to move to the next inhabitable planet, where surely the same destruction would come about. And even then, we might still pride ourselves on being "superior" to the rest of nature.

The illusion of our separation from nature, which we are actually inherently connected to, shows up in many ways:

- We no longer *grow* our food, we *buy it* in the grocery store
- We *own* other animals as pets
- We live in houses with fences or gates *guarding us and our belongings*
- We wear shoes that *separate* our feet from the ground beneath us
- We buy land, thinking *it belongs to us*, rather than *us belonging to the land*
- We take what we *want*, instead of simply what we *need*

Eckhart Tolle asks, "When this delusion of utter separateness underlies and governs whatever I think, say, and do, what kind of world do I create? To find the answer to this, observe how humans relate to each other, read a history book, or watch the news on television tonight."[90]

Have we ever stopped to think what might happen if we destroy all the resources needed to attain the first, physical base of Maslow's hierarchy of needs? What happens if we no longer have clean water to drink, non-toxic food to eat, or air that doesn't make us sick? What happens when we no longer have any sense of connection to nature, the source of life? What happens when we disrupt the delicate balance of the web of life?

One result is that we, and the rest of life on this planet, become ill—physically and mentally. Regardless of technological improvements, the more we have estranged ourselves from nature, the more ridden with death and disease we have become.

"Over a billion people, about 15 percent of the world's population, have some form of disability," according to the World Health Organization.[91] "One in four people in the world will be affected by mental or neurological disorders at some point in their lives."[92] That's almost 2 *billion* people suffering from mental disorders, despite medical advancements!

---

90 Tolle, Eckhart. 2005. A New Earth. London: Penguin.
91 "Disability And Health." 2019. Who.Int.
92 "WHO | Mental Disorders Affect One In Four People." 2019. Who. Int.

People are consequently treated with improper diagnosis, medications filled with synthetic chemicals or hormones, and invasive surgeries. Many *never* go on to actually get better, and that ill health and sense of helplessness negatively affects every aspect of life.

People can then become trapped in their unhappy life situations, which continues to *benefit* those who profit from controlled and distorted narratives. Meaning, sick people will always reach for things that might make them feel happy, however short-lived—whether it be religion, medication, food, clothes, or a shiny new sports car.

We continue to fill our inner voids with more consumption, and so the cycle continues.

***

As sad, scary, unfair, cruel, or hopeless as the propagation of this storyline might feel, the world is always transforming.

Daniel Quinn believed we could think ourselves out of our population explosion and subsequent planetary destruction. In *Ishmael,* he said, "At one billion I think it very likely that you might be able to live on here for … millions of years, without destroying the life of the world and yourselves with it … As a mere beginning of hope for you, a very decisive mental adaptation must be made to end that growth ... You're a tremendously inventive people, aren't you? Then *invent.*"[93]

Imagine what we all could do simply by readjusting our minds and focusing our thoughts a specific way. By harnessing knowledge and using clearly focused intention, we could input our time and energy into creating not just a better future, but a happier NOW.

But how does one go about changing the entire storyline of modern humanity, if he or she is just *one person*?

---

93   Quinn, Daniel. 1992. Ishmael.

CHAPTER 7:

BECOMING AN AUTHOR

"The old scripts have failed us … The old system is broken beyond repair. Our real point of power is not to go to war with the old, but rather upgrade our beliefs and understandings, to transform ourselves, and to make new consequential choices."

—RICHARD GORDON[94]

A new, cohesive storyline for the collective, global humanity is not necessary—awareness is enough. "Awareness is the greatest agent for change," said Tolle.[95] And your awareness has already shifted as an effect of reading the previous chapters.

---

94 Gordon, Richard. 2017. Secret Nature Of Matter.
95 Tolle, Eckhart. 2005. A New Earth. London: Penguin.

Rather than instating a new and improved collective narrative, we must simply begin to write our *own.* "Start telling a better-feeling story about the things that are important to you. Do not write your story like a factual documentary, writing the pros and cons of your existence, but instead tell the uplifting, fanciful, magical story of the wonder of your own life and see what happens. It will feel like magic as your life begins to transform before your eyes," said Esther Hicks, American inspirational speaker and author.[96]

I believe all that is necessary for positive global change is for more people to be aware and willing to help themselves. Get a clear focus on what your heart wants to happen in *only your own* story.

Hill wanted for people to "be true to themselves at all times and, since they cannot please everybody, therefore, to do a good job of pleasing themselves."[97] This idea might sound selfish initially. I assure you it is not.

The best thing you can do for others is to be genuinely happy.

If people can be fulfilled with who they are and find happiness from within, they may cease to:

96 "Abraham-Hicks." 2019. Facebook.Com.
97 Hill, Napoleon, Sharon L Lechter, Mark Victor Hansen, and Michael Bernard Beckwith. 2011. Outwitting The Devil.

- Blame others for their own unhappiness
- Reach for external validation
- Attempt to, consciously or unconsciously, manipulate or control others for self-gain
- Consume or purchase things to fill a void.

I believe that we can change the world simply by following our hearts. We can empower ourselves to become the authors of our own stories, instead of continually being pushed around by the thoughts of others. "Your purpose in life is to find your purpose and give your whole heart and soul to it,"—according to Buddha.[98]

***

Steve Jobs took over the world with his vision of electronics. He is no longer alive, but he is still running this show, regardless.

Many of us know that the person who has an Android instead of an iPhone gets picked on by their friends. That person probably goes to bed at night thinking about how they are missing out on group texts. Maybe they wish they had better camera quality.

---

98 Juma, Norbert. 2019. "60 Buddha Quotes About Life, Death, Peace, And Love." Everyday Power.

Because of Jobs and Apple, "selfie" was the Oxford Dictionary's word of the year in 2013.[99] There is now an app for absolutely everything, and humans are officially, in the words of Elon Musk, "cyborgs."[100]

Seven hundred million people worldwide now live holding a piece of Steve Jobs in our hands every single day of our lives.[101] There is something we can learn from him and apply to our new, personal narratives or life stories: Jobs said, "Intuition is a very powerful thing, more powerful than intellect."[102]

He gave away his secret of success in his 2005 Stanford commencement address, stating, "Much of what I stumbled into by following my curiosity and intuition turned out to be priceless later on."[103]

You're probably thinking:

- *What does he mean by that?*
- *Just because it worked for him does not mean it'll work for me.*

99 'Selfie' Named As Word Of The Year." 2013. BBC News.
100 "Why Elon Musk Thinks We're Already Cyborgs." 2019. Big Think.
101 "Here's How Many Iphones Are Currently Being Used Worldwide." 2019. Fortune.
102 Umoh, Ruth. 2019. "Steve Jobs And Albert Einstein Both Attributed Their Extraordinary Success To This Personality Trait." CNBC.
103 "Steve Jobs' 2005 Stanford Commencement Address." 2019. Forbes. Com.

- *That kind of thing is one-in-a-million, right?*
- *His heart and interests just happened to align with the creation of a genius invention. I can't do that.*

Well, Einstein also once noted, "The only real valuable thing is intuition." He was a walking genius. The man discovered how matter and energy warp the fabric of space-time to create the force of gravity.[104]

So why would Einstein give more credit to his heart and intuition than to his analytical brain? I think the answer to that is simple: *He must have known something we do not.*

According to the HeartMath Institute, a nonprofit research and education organization helping to establish heart-based living, *our heart's intelligence* is designed to help us make more intelligent decisions. "Not only does the heart respond to the brain, but the brain continuously responds to the heart."[105]

The heart is the first organ each one of us develops in the womb. It is like an internal antennae. To live in tune with what your heart communicates to you by way of feelings is to live under the guidance of your intuition—the most

104 Contributor, Tim. 2019. "Right Again, Einstein! Wobbling Pulsar Confirms General Relativity." Livescience.Com.
105 "The Science Of Heartmat.h. 2019.

invisibly intelligent part of yourself, which is always invisibly communicating with the world around you.

Napoleon Hill taught that the "sixth sense is the organ ... through which one receives all information ... which do not come through one or more of the five physical senses ... One can, through this same physical organ, contact and receive information from the universal storehouse known as Infinite Intelligence." He wanted people to gain "use of the sixth sense through which ideas present themselves in their minds from unknown sources, and to examine all such ideas carefully."[106]

The HeartMath Institute says that the intuitive, energetic heart is what people often call their "inner voice."[107] I believe this is what Jobs, Einstein, and Hill meant when they talked about:

- Curiosity
- Intuition
- The "other self"
- Sixth sense
- Infinite Intelligence

These are all words for what I had been calling Magic.

---

106 Hill, Napoleon, Sharon L Lechter, Mark Victor Hansen, and Michael Bernard Beckwith. 2011. Outwitting The Devil.
107 "The Science Of Heartmath." 2019.

The HeartMath Institute's research explains how the heart has an aura, or energy field, and an intelligence that can be read and felt by other people's brains and hearts. It is always beating, pulsating out, and affecting your environment, though you cannot see it—and likely had no idea it was happening.[108]

HeartMath continues on to say, "When you shift into a coherent state, your heart and brain work together, reducing stress, and increasing cognitive function and intuitive discernment … Genuine emotions of compassion or appreciation increase heart coherence, benefiting people, animals, and the environment." Coherence is harmony in our psychological *and* physiological body processes—a state of optimal function.[109]

Research also shows that a lack of genuine heart connection underlies a significant amount of stress we experience, as was mentioned in Maslow's pyramid of human needs.[110] On the other hand, "Intentional connection … increases our sense of self-security, creates clearer choices, and gives easier access to our heart's intuitive guidance, along with

---

108 Ibid.
109 Ibid.
110 Childre, Doc. 2019. "Renewing Heart Qualities."

lifting the spirit of others and the environment," says the HeartMath Institute.[111]

To live with a sense of connection, rather than separation, is to live in tune with your heart. To live in tune with your heart and its gentle guidance is to walk hand-in-hand with Magic.

***

Your intuition speaks to you, and you can feel it when it does. You can also feel when you're listening to your intuition and when you're not.

Today, most of us *are not listening.* Many of us live in a constant battle between head and heart. Most of the time, our intuition gets overruled and tuned out entirely.

We tend to listen instead to facts, to others, and to the thoughts that are largely conditioned by our past. Our egos are running the show both individually and collectively— controlling us most of the time without us even being aware of the damage it is doing.

One can certainly feel the difference between making heart-decisions and brain-decisions, though. Napoleon Hill explained

---

111 "The Science Of Heartmath." 2019.

this in *Outwitting the Devil*, saying that "two entities occupy your body, as in fact two similar entities occupy the body of each living person on earth."[112] He called them fear and faith. I equate fear to your brain, and faith to your heart.

Napoleon explains that faith, the heart, "performs no miracles," but that "it will guide you when you call on it." He is sure to tell readers that your heart's intuition "will not do your work for you; it will only guide you intelligently in achieving for yourself the objects of your desires."[113] Listening to what your heart is communicating to you and following through on its genuine needs and desires puts you in a spot for Magic to guide you from within and affect your life on many levels.

To paraphrase Alan Watts, a British philosopher, love is what you are at the core.[114] When you take proper care of yourself and genuinely listen to your heart, your love can flow more openly. When you will not *let that love out*, it instead turns into something of self-sabotage.

I know that following your heart and your intuition can feel like a huge risk at times—it will often ask you to make leaps

---

112 Hill, Napoleon, Sharon L Lechter, Mark Victor Hansen, and Michael Bernard Beckwith. 2011. Outwitting The Devil.
113 Ibid.
114 "Alan Watts How To Stop Being Self Conscious." 2019. Youtube.

without knowing what is in front of you. But that space just outside of your immediate comfort zone is where all the Magic can begin to happen.

Dr. Nicole LePera, psychologist, told a story once of a bird in a cage. Though the bird was trapped, it began to feel accustomed to the cage. Consequently, once the door of the cage opened, it was too afraid to fly freely—it was afraid of what might lie beyond its walls. The cage began to feel safe for the bird, and so it stayed.[115]

The bird is your heart, the cage is your mind. Let yourself be free. Take a risk and follow your heart. Ray Bradbury, author of *Fahrenheit 451*, urges you to "jump and build your wings on the way down."[116]

Risks are important. By trusting your intuition and life's mysterious ways, despite any feelings of discomfort, chaos, or confusion, one can learn valuable lessons and be led into invaluable life experiences. I have leapt for the past year from one risk to the next, not entirely knowing where my heart would take me.

---

115 LePera, Nicole. 2019. "The Holistic Psychologist – The Power To Heal Yourself." The Holistic Psychologist.

116 Bridges, Lawrence. 2019. "A Conversation With Ray Bradbury." Youtube.

In the summer of 2018, I started telling people that I was writing a book—a *huge* claim for somebody not actually writing a book. But putting myself out there like that, like my heart wanted me to, somehow worked for me. I opened myself up, became vulnerable, got external encouragement, and gained mentors.

One of my mentors said, "When you write a best-seller, I want it signed on my desk."

Maybe those events were coincidental, but then again, maybe not. As I took baby steps toward fulfilling an ultimate dream of mine, life seemed to cheer me on.

I admit, this entire book is a risk—and a huge one. I do not know what may come about on behalf of this book. I do not know what my peers, especially those who still identify as Mormon, will think while reading this book.

But here I am, still writing it, on behalf of my heart's guidance.

And I fully believe that, had this particular chance to write my own book not materialized for me, this book would still have come about another way. It's just that I so happened to follow my intuition and take the risk the *first* time the opportunity presented itself.

***

Betting on yourself, *one single person*, to help rewrite the stories that have been plaguing humanity and this planet for so long probably feels like a *giant* risk… . But it's one that's worth every scary second. Your personal narrative being one you actually enjoy living is *crucial*.

Living life on this Earth is like being put on a limitless playground. You get to do anything you dream of here, if you simply let yourself. You *can* choose to empower yourself—despite the directions some narratives urge you to follow—and do what genuinely benefits your happiness, and therefore benefiting others.

I earnestly think that following our heart's guidance is the *one* way we can rewrite the story of humanity—to become like children again, in tune with the Magic, and do only what we love. We are allowed to let ourselves stop taking ourselves and life so seriously, and to play a little more.

Life should be *fun*. It is to be experienced, not controlled or dreaded or feared.

If each person were to take charge of their own hearts and own lives—if the world was filled with people more willing to help themselves, and more intent on listening to their inner voices—I believe we would *all* be healthier and happier.

Many would finally learn through the process of risk-taking that the negative stories, worries, or doubts in their head never do happen. People would learn that fears mostly never come true, and they could continue to listen to their intuition more fearlessly in time.

People would become free of that crippling or paralyzing fear, able to do now what they want to deep down in their heart and soul. And a world filled with people willing to do the work *for themselves* and make the choices that their hearts desire would, indeed, be a more harmonious one. People would finally be free of certain egoic behaviors, like:

- Dressing in clothes you hate to impress people you don't like
- Committing to relationships that don't truly fulfill you
- Working jobs that drain you of life, energy, and happiness
- Posting edited photos on social media for likes that momentarily raise your feelings of self-worth
- Engaging in activities that you do not truly enjoy

Of all the people who are doing what they *truly love* with all of their hearts, which of them is:

- Angry?
- Stressed?
- Unfulfilled?
- Unhappy with life or with others?
- Consuming in order to fill an internal void?

When your heart and brain are working in unison, you are affecting every single person in the world, whether you know it or not. Like HeartMath said, your heart radiates out and affects your environment.[117] Your actions also affect others, so they should be taken from a place of love and intuition rather than logic and fear.

One person is like a drop in an ocean—but each drop can surely make an everlasting ripple. The choice to make this mental adaptation is in your hands. Just think: In the story called "My Life," where is the main character? Ask yourself:

- *What chapter am I in?*
- *Am I happy here?*
- *Do I want this part of my story to end?*
- *How could I make the next chapter better?*
- *What is my heart telling me?*

---

117 "The Science Of Heartmath." 2019.

Actually answer these. Think about it. Maybe take out a pen and paper and write it down. Think of yourself now as the *author* rather than the main character. *This is where your power lies.*

You are no longer a character, lost in a story. You are the author, directing the protagonist's every move. You write the main character's lines. You get to decide the hero's course of action.

You control what story the main character lives in. Make your story one you *love*.

***

Because when you do the things you want to do, things that give you joy, you can become truly happy. You can also, among other things:

- Bless others
- Smile
- Become generous
- Act lightheartedly
- Laugh
- Trust others
- Become more honest in return
- Invite genuine heart-to-heart connection

The HeartMath Institute says "true connection at the heart level organically creates a pathway to coherent cooperation and more effective outcomes."[118] But don't simply take their word for it. Experiment with it yourself.

You might find that, when you're genuinely happy because you're doing things you genuinely want to be doing, that positive energy rubs off onto the people around you. It may actually put the people you interact with in a better mood, and smooth over problems more easily. People might start to want to be around you more, or you may start to attract other loving and lighthearted people into your life.

Soon enough, others might start to carry that infectious energy of yours on with them and spread it around. Your state of happiness that stemmed from doing what you actually wanted to can now ripple through your friends, family, and community.

Love is powerful. Your intuition is a bad-ass. It's about time you start listening to it.

Trust it—it knows what it is doing. By empowering yourself, you allow others to empower themselves as well. And when you *do* finally step into your heart's power, you become the

---

118 Ibid.

true and powerful author of your story—curating your life to be exactly the way your heart wishes.

The universal Magic, once you are acting in accordance with your heart's gentle guidance, will start to notice the risks you are taking and send you assistance—in sometimes odd, unexpected, or surprising ways. It'll begin to cheer you on, just as it did me.

When you become so in tune with your heart's guidance, life really does stop giving you hell and becomes your partner. People who act in accordance to their intuition, like Steve Jobs or Einstein, can become the authors of their life stories as well as make miraculous creations and discoveries—*things that forever change the course of history on this Earth.*

Now, it's your turn.

CHAPTER 8:

THE FOUR PS OF PRACTICAL MAGIC

"All other creatures move in response to definite laws of nature. Man alone defies nature's laws ... "

—NAPOLEON HILL[119]

You, as an author, have the power over every choice your character makes.

However, many authors have gotten lost in the roles of their protagonist—we have taken our character's lives so seriously that we have forgotten we are the ones creating it. Many have

---

119 Hill, Napoleon, Sharon L Lechter, Mark Victor Hansen, and Michael Bernard Beckwith. 2011. Outwitting The Devil.

forgotten that they are the ones in control of their life situation, rather than their life situation being in control of them.

In order to become the rightful authors of our own stories, we must learn the true nature of the world around us and adapt to the way it works. By understanding the ways of the universe, we can work in harmony with its laws to better create our own stories. Napoleon Hill stated, "Nature's law is, 'Know what you want, adapt yourself to my laws, and you shall have it.'"[120]

Through my years of reading and research, I learned much about the workings of people and nature alike. Between self-help books, ancient religious texts, quantum physics, environmental science and psychology, I pieced together the most useful bits of those laws to form my own lifeline—*The Four Ps of Practical Magic.*

These guidelines are what I use to better adapt myself to the laws of the universe. They help me to guide my thoughts and actions, which inevitably helps me reach my goals as well as create my own life story. Each guideline helps me to better remember the connection in all things, to trust life's timing, and to use my mind in a way that will attract success to me. My actions therefore become more powerful and filled with purpose.

---

120 Ibid.

The greater perspective that these four guidelines open you up to can allow you to influence yourself, and your environment, in a Magical way.

***

1. PERPETUAL ENERGY AND MAGNETISM

The Secret Nature of Matter taught me that matter is 99.99 percent empty space, or energy. The physical world we see and interact with makes up the remaining less than .01 percent of existence.[121] You, too, are made up of more space than physical presence.[122]

Our lives depend more on the state of these invisible, energetic realms than the things physically showing up around us. Our thoughts and emotions are powerful energies. Energy can never be created nor destroyed, only transmuted—therefore we cannot fake or deny emotions, only work to transform them.

Every specific thing in existence has its own energetic signature, made up of vibrations. Each signature vibrates at its own particular frequency. Similar vibrational frequencies will be attracted to each other, like a magnet.

---

121 Gordon, Richard. 2017. Secret Nature Of Matter.
122 "20 Amazing Facts About The Human Body." 2019. The Guardian.

Every emotion and thought has its own specific vibrational frequency. Therefore, what you think and feel the most strongly and frequently about, you will inevitably attract toward you. Abraham Hicks says, "As you think you vibrate, as you vibrate you attract."[123] You are always creating your life and experiences based on the dominant ways that you think and feel.

If you spend most of your time thinking about how lonely you are, your life will become empty. If you think only about how successful you are, your life will become positive and filled with opportunity. If you constantly feel like a victim, life will give you more situations that you feel victimized within.

Energy not only attracts your dominant thoughts and feelings toward you, it has the power to make you feel magnetized toward or utterly repelled by people that do or do not match your own energetic signature. Napoleon Hill explained, in the case of being magnetized toward a person, "brains attuned to the same rate of thought vibrations can easily and quickly exercise the privilege of entering and inspecting each other's filing cabinets of thoughts."[124]

---

123 "Abraham Hicks You Are Always Manifesting." 2019. Pinterest.
124 Hill, Napoleon, Sharon L Lechter, Mark Victor Hansen, and Michael Bernard Beckwith. 2011. Outwitting The Devil.

The interaction of vibrational frequencies is why you may feel like you "vibe" with one person and not the next. It is also why you may get a "bad vibe" from someone instantly upon meeting. Always trust the vibes.

***

Perpetual energy and magnetism reminds me that there are forces at work and things in existence beyond what I can see. It reminds me that I can't cast off thoughts or emotions, but that I have the power to transmute, or change, any thoughts or feelings within me.

This guideline helps me remember that I cannot feel sad and still expect to attract or experience the feeling of happiness. It reminds me to use the technique of "vibrational matching" to create my dream reality. I practice consistently thinking the thoughts and feeling the emotions I desire more of in my life, therefore attracting what I want toward me.

Finally, perpetual energy and magnetism also teaches me to recognize when I feel uneasy around certain people, things, or situations. I now know to trust that initial gut feeling—if our energy does not align, I should step away from that situation and move toward things I actually do "vibe" with.

2. PATTERNS AND REFLECTIONS

"As above, so below; as within, so without."[125]

Life is full of patterns and reflections. *Everything* is connected to *everything*. All things on earth are a manifestation of the same *one* source—the quantum, universal mind we talked about in chapter four. We are all smaller parts of a grander whole, and can see aspects of ourselves in all of existence.

There is an overarching regularity to our world, shown in the patterns, designs, reflections, and cycles found in everything around us. There are patterns that mirror each other all throughout nature, from the infinitely large to the infinitely small. A few cosmic examples include:

- Our brain cells looking like clusters of galaxies
- The mathematical golden ratio being found everywhere from plants to shells to hurricane formations
- The makeup of an atom, consisting of mostly space with some revolving protons and electrons, imitating the makeup of our solar system with its revolving planets

Likewise, life mirrors what you feel internally—as within, so without. What you feel and think turns into what you see and experience. We must accept what life is showing to

---

125 Staff, Gaia. 2018. "As Above So Below; Alchemy And The Emerald Tablet." Gaia.

us, because it is only a reflection of who and what we are at that time.

This reflection from life is where *synchronicity* can come into play—meaningful coincidences. Life will reflect to you the things that are taking place within you. For example, I remember seeing rhinos *everywhere*—something that usually doesn't happen all that often—just after applying to the job in South Africa.

There is also a regularity in the rhythm of cycles, like how:

- Summer turns to winter, back to summer
- The moon goes new to full to new again
- We go from day to night to day again

As such, humans have their own regular cycles that we utilize to function optimally. A few examples include how:

- We sleep, wake up, and sleep again
- We eat and release waste on a loop
- An average woman has a regular monthly cycle

We also experience energy cycles—times where things are stagnant, and times when life is exciting. Just as nature goes through a cold and dead winter, we all have darker cycles that we go through, too—and that is perfectly normal. These low times go on to be something you learn from, becoming the catalyst for your next high-energy period of growth and abundance.

***

Patterns and reflections remind me that I am a part of a grander universe, which is intelligently designed. It helps me to trust life's rhythm and patterns, and to ride the inevitable waves, as change is the only constant. It teaches me to look for connections, and to see myself in others.

This guideline also reminds me that my life is only a reflection of what's going on within me. I can, therefore, direct my thoughts and feelings in a positive way, to shift the way I experience life. It also reminds me that life is always guiding me and teaching me more about myself.

Lastly, it helps me to not get overwhelmed or trapped by slower or less fulfilling parts of my individual cycle, and to stay strong in knowing that it will pass in time. It also teaches me to revel in the good while it lasts and be grateful for the learning experiences given by the "bad." Patterns and reflections remind me not to doubt myself or my experiences, because there is a regularity behind all things.

3. PERCEPTION AND PERSPECTIVE

Everything in this world seemingly has its opposite. There is a contrast to things, such as:

- Night and day
- Hot and cold
- Male and female
- Happy and sad

It is important to know that one is never better than the other; both opposing forces are important aspects of existence. Opposites have their proper place, and they teach us perspective, like in the way that:

- We experience darkness to get a sense of light
- We feel hot in order to understand cold
- We need both masculine and feminine energies to give balance to one another
- Sadness gives a nice contrast to happiness

After all, happiness would get boring after a while if it was the only thing ever felt—yet we tend to label sadness as "bad." The idea of "bad versus good" is only a product of perception. What one may call bad, another may call good.

We *can* use the idea of opposition to our benefit, though, by knowing that anything undesirable in our experience also has an achievable opposite. The pendulum will always swing the other way, no matter how great or how horrible things get. However, there *is* always good in the bad, just as there is bad in the good.

We can also use perspective to understand the idea that all is relative. Everything is neutral until *we* assign meaning to it. While one may love yellow for reminding them of sunshine, another may hate it for reminding them of urine.

Any judgement, comparison, or label is a result of our own perception of things, and we have the power to change our own perception at any time. When we attach associations to things, they can then hold an illusory sense of power and meaning—positive or negative. In objective reality, nothing holds any meaning, all things just simply exist.

We can use a new perspective to gain a clearer view of our lives, thoughts, and emotions, which will help change our previous perceptions.

***

Perception and perspective teach me that contrast is necessary to have the beauty of the whole picture. It reminds me to value each thing in my experience, rather than immediately judging or labeling it. It also teaches me that any opinion or judgement I have is only an illusion of my own perception.

This guideline also reminds me that, even at my lowest, there are good times of an equal magnitude awaiting me. It teaches me that the bad and the good go hand in hand and that there is good in every experience—sometimes I may just have to work a little harder to find it.

I also use perception and perspective to realize that my negative experiences are not necessarily bad, I have simply judged it to be that way. Another trick I use is to compare my situation to one that I would absolutely hate to be in, and then by changing my perception I suddenly feel grateful for my situation rather than trapped by it.

Finally, this guideline reminds me that judging or comparing myself or my life with others is a waste of time. Any judgement I give to something only gives it more power over me. This guideline encompasses a way to go through life with more acceptance and compassion—nothing is good, nothing is bad, all is merely existing.

4. PARTICIPATION

You must participate in life in order to get results. Though you can use your thoughts and emotions to attract what you want toward you, you must still put in the work to see your goals manifest physically. The energetic universe is Magical, but it is not a genie that grants your mind's every wish.

Your actions must also be in alignment with your thoughts or wishes. Every action you take also acts as a boomerang— what you put out into the universe, it will deliver right back to you.

Ralph Waldo Emerson, a transcendentalist philosopher, said in his essay *Compensation* that each person is compensated in like manner for that which he or she has contributed.[126] You will be repaid for the time and effort (or lack thereof) invested into your actions.

It is also important to participate in ways which benefit you and others. With every action you take, you send a rippling chain reaction throughout the universe. What you think, say, and do affects every last thing in existence, near or far.

Napoleon Hill said, "Often the cause is so far removed from the effect that the circumstance can be explained only by attributing it to the operation of luck ... The terms "luck" and "miracle" are twin sisters. Neither of them has any real

---

126 Emerson, Ralph Waldo. 2019. "The Law Of Compensation." Brian-tracy.Com.

existence except in the imaginations of people … Remember this: everything having a real existence is capable of proof."[127]

Every cause has an effect, and every effect a cause, regardless of the separation of time or space between the two. This means that absolutely nothing happens by coincidence. Participation gives you the power to send out your own unique ripple, with certainty that it will make a difference now as well as down the line.

The world would not be the same as it is today without you in it.

***

Participation makes me aware of what I am doing, reminding to take proper action that aligns with my goals and dreams. I know now that the effort I put out will always come back to me, which is my motivation to keep pushing, even though results take time. It also wakes me up to the fact that every experience is a making of my own creation—even the bad ones. I had to act on its behalf for it to show up in my life.

This guideline keeps me conscious of the fact that all of *my* actions do in fact affect others in ways unimaginable. It points out to me that what I do *now* will undeniably affect

---

127 Hill, Napoleon, Sharon L Lechter, Mark Victor Hansen, and Michael Bernard Beckwith. 2011. Outwitting The Devil.

those who come after me, and so I must think ahead as well as act wisely and with care. I can actually use my actions to benefit myself as well as others.

And lastly, this guideline reminds me that nothing is coincidental. It puts me in the power over my own decisions, as well as it makes me the only person I can credit for my consequences—both negative and positive. It reminds me not to blame myself, but to continually try to be better.

***

Doing your best to adjust yourself to the Four Ps of Practical Magic is a game-changer. They will always help you adjust your perspective, gain a greater sense of meaning, and help you get through hard times. The laws will help you to think, feel, and act on behalf of your purpose, with confidence that there is a greater Magic out there responding to your own energetic signature.

In short, these are the main takeaways of the practical four Ps:

- Perpetual Energy and Magnetism:
  - Everything in existence is made up of energy, frequency, and vibration
  - Energy cannot be created or destroyed, only transmuted

- You can attract what you want by thinking and feeling it consistently
- Patterns and Reflections:
  - All things come from the same source
  - Your life is a reflection of your internal world
  - There is a rhythm to the universe which maintains perfect balance
- Perception and Perspective:
  - All things have their opposite
  - Yet, everything is merely relative—everything just *is*
- Participation:
  - Every cause has an effect
  - You will always be compensated for your actions—or lack thereof
  - You must take action to get results

PART III:

These remaining chapters focus on the different aspects of a human being, guiding you to become healthier and stronger in each area. Because holistic health empowers one to better author their life story, each topic lists practical tools to help you align with Magic and tap into your own heart and intuition. It teaches you how to retrain your brain, take back your power over your body, and become more in tune with yourself and the world outside of you. I encourage you to do your own research as well as to practice the things that stand out to you.

CHAPTER 9:

PHYSICAL

___

" … there is no problem which does not have an appropriate solution and the solution often may be found in the circumstance creating the problem."

—NAPOLEON HILL[128]

The first step of Maslow's pyramid of needs is physical, and this chapter will help you to master that base step. Though what we physically see is the smallest portion of existence, I think it is the best starting point—especially as the focus of the following chapters is mainly invisible. When you can actually *see* the changes you're making, it can be easier to feel like you are, in fact, making progress.

___

128 Hill, Napoleon, Sharon L Lechter, Mark Victor Hansen, and Michael
Bernard Beckwith. 2011. Outwitting The Devil.

The topics in this chapter affect you as well as affect the environment. Everyone is different, so take the pieces of advice that work best for *you* and try to implement them gradually.

INFLUENCE AND CONNECTION

Humans are social beings. Who you will inevitably become has much to do with your inner circle of influence. Jim Rohn, American entrepreneur, said that we are the average of the five people we spend the most time with.[129]

Napoleon Hill said, "The most important part of one's environment is that created by his association with others. All people absorb and take over, either consciously or unconsciously, the thought-habits of those with whom they associate closely … Nothing contributes more to one's success and happiness than carefully chosen associates."[130]

Take notice of the people you spend the most time with and determine how they may be affecting you. It is OK to pull some closer to you or move others away from you, depending on the influence they have. Ask yourself:

---

129 Groth, Aimee. 2019. "You're The Average Of The Five People You Spend The Most Time With." Business Insider.
130 Hill, Napoleon, Sharon L Lechter, Mark Victor Hansen, and Michael Bernard Beckwith. 2011. Outwitting The Devil.

- *Who do I spend my time with?*
- *How are they influencing me?*
- *Should I spend more or less time around them?*
- *What type of influence would benefit me?*
- *Who can I spend time with that will have a positive influence on me?*

Once you determine those answers, you can now Participate. Be selective with who you spend your time with, and watch your life shift accordingly.

SOCIAL MEDIA INFLUENCE

Because many of us are now living largely through social media, the above lesson of influence also applies to the online world. Social media has largely become a scheme for "clout-chasers," and influencers often look as if they are living larger than life, though it can be very deceiving.

A social media persona is likely a highlight reel—the way one wishes to be seen by the world. This has sometimes been unhealthy, with people engaging in behaviors such as:

- Curating a fake life to get likes or followers
- Photoshopping photos to achieve that "dream" body
- Masking debt, depression, or eating disorders

Matty Mo, known as The Most Famous Artist, wrote, "I started getting off on the images I posted of myself ... Feeling a little zap of pleasure with each additional "like." But I was feeding the beast."[131] Many today have become addicted to social media. Others have started to derive their self-worth and identities from their online profiles, or have gone down the dark hole of comparison and inadequacy.

On the other hand, social media *can* be channeled into something useful. I've seen Instagram turn people into:

- Artists
- Musicians
- Thought leaders
- Fitness trainers
- Spiritual gurus
- Life coaches

Social media can be tools for growth or weapons of destruction, depending on how you navigate them. Ask yourself:

- *Who am I following?*
- *Are those people benefitting me in any way?*
- *How are the people on my feed making me feel about myself?*

---

131 Mo, Matty. 2019. "War & Porn: Becoming An Avatar." Medium.

Take stock of these answers, and unfollow anyone causing you negativity. Choose to surround yourself with only uplifting content and people that inspire you.

SOCIAL MEDIA BEHAVIOR

Instagram, Facebook, Snapchat, YouTube, and even LinkedIn or MySpace can also be used as a sort of diary. They have been around long enough to go back and reflect on your time there. Users can observe their digital history to analyze details and find patterns in their own behavior, as well as take note of special experiences and memories. Try taking note of things like:

- How you've grown and changed throughout your online experience
- How many beautiful places and moments you have seen
- What you have taken special interest in over the years

With these virtual time capsules, you can easily discover your online behaviors, feelings, and interests. The things you follow, share, or post online are very real needs and desires. Once aware of them, you can start to incorporate more of these things into your *real* life.

Social media can be a wonderful tool for expression, creativity and connection. It is simply important not to get swept away in the falsity of it. Take a step back and disconnect in order to connect with what really matters. It will never hurt to ask yourself:

- *How am I presenting myself to the online world?*
- *Am I being authentic, or portraying a persona?*
- *How can I incorporate aspects of that persona into my real life?*
- *How can I gain confidence in being more authentic online?*

NATURE AND GROUNDING

Humans used to live in nature, as a part of nature. Ancient tribes will say that the land does not belong to them, but that they belong to the land.[132] Throughout history, we lived *on* the earth. We walked on it, slept on it, ate from it.

Today, we live inside of houses. When outside, we wear shoes with rubber soles. Many of us live in cities with zero connection to nature.

But nature is *mandatory* for our wellbeing. An Oxford study stated that, "Human beings are part of natural ecosystems and depend on them for their survival … In an urbanized

---

132 Drywater-Whitekiller, Virginia. 2019. "We Belong To The Land: Native Americans Experiencing And Coping With Racial Micro-aggressions." Questia.Com

world, the role of ecosystems for our survival is perhaps only peripherally perceived."[133]

Humans are, indeed, unaware that a connection with nature is needed to maintain mental and physical wellbeing. The Journal of Environmental and Public Health states, "The research suggests that this disconnect may be a major contributor to physiological dysfunction and unwellness."[134] Benefits of spending time in nature include:

- Improved mood
- Reduced stress or anger
- Improved physical health
- Improved confidence and self-esteem
- Being more active
- Making new connections[135]

An incredible finding from the Journal of Environmental and Public Health shows that, "Omnipresent throughout the environment is a surprisingly beneficial, yet overlooked

133 van den Bosch, Matilda. 2017. "Natural Environments, Health, And Well-Being." Oxford Research Encyclopedia.
134 Chevalier, Gaétan, Stephen T. Sinatra, James L. Oschman, Karol Sokal, and Pawel Sokal. 2012. "Earthing: Health Implications Of Reconnecting The Human Body To The Earth's Surface Electrons." Journal Of Environmental And Public Health
135 "Nature And Mental Health." 2019. Mind.Org.Uk.

global resource for health maintenance, disease prevention, and clinical therapy: the surface of the Earth itself."[136]

Humans are electrical systems and the Earth is a natural source of electrons. The Earth's natural electrons transfer from the ground into the body when we touch its surface. Its "negative potential can create a stable internal bioelectrical environment for the normal functioning of all body systems."[137]

It is crucial to develop a connection with nature, and it can be done easily by incorporating small activities like:

- Going barefoot in grass
- Growing or picking food
- Bringing nature indoors
- Connecting with animals
- Going for a picnic in the park
- Listening to nature sounds

---

136 Chevalier, Gaétan, Stephen T. Sinatra, James L. Oschman, Karol Sokal, and Pawel Sokal. 2012. "Earthing: Health Implications Of Reconnecting The Human Body To The Earth's Surface Electrons." Journal Of Environmental And Public Health

137 Ibid.

MONEY

Money is simply a physical form of energy. Contrary to popular belief, money is not evil, nor does it buy happiness. But it can buy opportunity and change, if used consciously.

Our capitalist society functions on the consumer. The consumer truly has all the power—without consumers, businesses have nothing. Keep this in mind when you are disappointed with a company, a CEO, their beliefs, or practices. Your money speaks!

Many things are purchased in order to feel less empty or to fill some sort of internal void—boredom, loneliness, perhaps jealousy. But the more conscious you become of how you are spending your money, where it is going, and what you are giving energy to, the healthier your relationship with money will become.

I used to go to the mall or take myself out to eat when I had a bad day. What I was unaware of at the time was how my "harmless spending" indirectly contributed to:

- Environmental destruction
- Use of toxic chemicals
- Pollution
- Child labor
- Animal abuse

- Climate change[138]

I learned that it is extremely important to pay attention to what you are buying. I no longer give money or energy to things that I do not believe in, that do not benefit me, or that put any harm into the world. If there is a change you wish to see in the world, put your money where your mouth is and let your money talk for you. Start paying attention to things like:

- Who or what you are giving your money and energy to
- How products affect yourself as well as the environment
- What the producers of the products you use are doing "behind the scenes"
- How you can use your spending to increase health and sustainability

And, at the end of the day, if you are low on financial energy, keep it to yourself! If you have financial energy to spare, then you can spend it on people and things you truly believe in.

PLASTIC

One of the ways money can be detrimental to this physical world is the energy given to production and consumption of plastic—especially single-use.

---

138 "Environmental Impacts Of The Fashion Industry." 2019. Sustainyourstyle.

Plastic is a giant contributor to pollution and aquatic devastation. It does not decompose easily—the Plastic Pollution Coalition says, "Plastic is a substance the earth cannot digest."[139]

Most recycled bits, including biodegradable and compostable plastics, don't actually make it to recycling or the ideal composting environments—it costs too much to collect and process. When they *do* start to decay, "A byproduct of their decay is methane, a greenhouse gas roughly thirty-times more potent than carbon dioxide."[140]

Environmental Health News says, "The degradation of plastic leads to microplastics that can get into people, wildlife, soil, and water."[141] It also affects your body. The Plastic Pollution Coalition says, "Plastic pollution is toxic to human health. Even babies are born pre-polluted."[142]

According to the Center for International Environmental Law, health problems associated with plastics include:

- Cancers
- Diabetes

---

139 "Frequently Asked Questions." 2019. Plastic Pollution Coalition.
140 Ibid.
141 "Plastic Threatens Our Health From Before Production To Long After It's Thrown Away: Report." 2019. EHN
142 "Frequently Asked Questions." 2019. Plastic Pollution Coalition.

- Several organ malfunctions
- Impact on eyes, skin and other sensory organs
- Birth defects[143]

In accordance with awareness of where your money is going, be aware of what you are buying that uses plastic. You can work to reduce overall plastic use by:

- Using glass cups, straws, dishes, jars, and storage containers
- Ordering less from online stores (yes, you'll have to stifle your Amazon addiction)
- Bringing reusable grocery bags to the market
- Buying produce instead of processed foods
- Purchasing produce in its natural packaging (skin) rather than plastic packaging
- Supporting companies that use plastic alternatives
- Being aware of your consumption and waste levels

BIRTH CONTROL

Birth control is extremely important for a species with an ever-growing population.

---

143 "Plastic Threatens Our Health From Before Production To Long After It'S Thrown Away: Report." 2019. EHN.

The expectation is for *women* to take sole responsibility over birth control. However, a woman can get pregnant *one time in a period of nine months*. A man, on the other hand, can impregnate an *unlimited amount of women within nine months*.

Unfair and impractical gender imbalances aside, one commonly used method of birth control today is an oral-contraceptive—pills made of synthetic (man-made) female hormones. These man-made hormones alter a female body's natural balance and have wide-ranging side effects, including:

- Nausea
- Irregular periods
- Headaches
- Weight change
- Sore breasts
- Mood changes[144]

It is hard for a woman to connect with the inherent Magic within and around her when her body is spending its energy processing synthetic hormones. It affects her ability to function physically, mentally, and emotionally. A Harvard Health study says, "All forms of hormonal contraception were

---

144 "Birth Control Pills: General Information." 2019. Center For Young Women's Health.

associated with an increased risk of developing depression
... "145

I experienced depression when I started using birth control. Crying was a daily activity. Having researched the link between birth control and anxiety or depression, I stopped using the pill and switched to a natural method. Some non-hormonal birth control alternatives include:

- The Daysy, a digital form of birth control that measures your basal body temperature and tracks your cycle
- Copper IUD
- Condoms
- Vasectomies for men—a minor, reversible surgery that blocks sperm from ejaculation

Men *should* participate in birth control, considering they can impregnate women at an exponential rate. A vasectomy prevents pregnancy better than any other method of birth control and does not affect orgasm.[146] Men can be kings who take a knee to help the queens in their lives flourish physically and mentally.

---

145 Tello, Monique. 2016. "Can Hormonal Birth Control Trigger Depression?" Harvard Health Blog.
146 "What Is A Vasectomy?" 2019. Urologyhealth.Org.

SEX

Napoleon Hill said, "It is not sex that is vulgar. It is the individual who neglects or refuses to control and guide it … The neglect is due to ignorance of the real nature of sex …"[147]

Sex has long been:

- Looked down upon
- Denied
- Repressed
- Seen as a sin before marriage
- Used as a tool for judgement of moral character

Human bodies have become things to hide, manipulate, or obsess over, rather than beautiful creations of God to admire and respect. Growing up Mormon, I was taught that a "sexually impure" woman was like a piece of chewed up gum, and that good men would never find her to be desirable.

I was never taught that sex was a natural form of expression to be shared between people who love and care about each other. I also never knew that love and caring could exist outside of marriage, or that it was not, in fact, a temptation from the devil. Sex can allow for spiritual unification and bonding at the deepest level.

---

147 Hill, Napoleon, Sharon L Lechter, Mark Victor Hansen, and Michael Bernard Beckwith. 2011. Outwitting The Devil.

The religious rule for sex only to be shared only between *married, heterosexual couples* has caused countless people to regard themselves as "bad" for having natural sexual desires. Many have denied themselves of sexual pleasure, which can come out in less beneficial ways. One result of sexual repression is higher pornography ratings, according to Marty Klein, sex therapist and psychotherapist. He says, "the highest per capita purchase of online porn is…Utah. Of course."[148]

Hill wanted people to, "Teach children the true nature and function of the emotion of sex … The desire for sex expression is as natural as the desire for food … If the emotion of sex is shut off from the natural mode of expression, it will break out in some other less desirable form."[149]

Sexual desire and expression is natural, healthy, and it should be welcomed in safe, trusting, and loving situations—just don't overindulge.

---

148 Klein, Marty. 2019. "Science Shows What Sexual Repression Actually Looks Like." Psychology Today.
149 Hill, Napoleon, Sharon L Lechter, Mark Victor Hansen, and Michael Bernard Beckwith. 2011. Outwitting The Devil.

ILLNESS

I was put on the medical merry-go-round from the age of about thirteen until now—nine years of bouncing around, clueless.

I went from doctor to doctor, all offering different diagnoses and explanations. Not a single one of them could agree on what was wrong, or what treatment was needed.

There are millions of Americans on this same loop, leading to "countless people feeling that their bodies aren't to be trusted ... that there's something wrong with them at the core ... They feel betrayed, defective, weak—when in fact it's just the opposite," Anthony William, the Medical Medium, states.[150]

"The diagnostic framework points blame in the wrong direction. It makes people think their bodies are betraying them. Once they stop trusting their bodies, they lose faith that they can heal ... You can heal."[151]

Your body is run by Magic and has an incredible healing ability, given the proper chance. Being sick is not a curse,

---

150 William, Anthony. 2017. Medical Medium Thyroid Healing.
151 Ibid.

though sometimes it can feel that way. Through experiences of ill health we have the ability to become more:

- Compassionate
- Grounded
- Humble
- Empathetic
- Wise

From a different perspective, "Our bodies have the ability to be sick, not as a dysfunction, but as a communication from our own higher self of how we have stopped loving," explained Richard Gordon.[152] We can use illness to learn how to better love ourselves, others, and our own bodies.

PLACEBO HEALING EFFECT

Our bodies miraculously react to the "placebo effect"—or to thoughts and beliefs you give yourself. And, yet, it seems that this superpower has been completely overlooked by most of the health care system. A Harvard Health study admits that, "Now science has found that under the right circumstances, a placebo can be just as effective as traditional treatments."[153]

---

152 Gordon, Richard. 2017. Secret Nature Of Matter.
153 Publishing, Harvard. 2019. "The Power Of The Placebo Effect." Harvard Health

Dr. Joe Dispenza, a researcher of quantum physics and neuroscience, says "Your nervous system is the greatest pharmacist in the world." By a person *believing* they are getting a treatment, "they begin to program their autonomic nervous system to create the exact pharmacy of chemicals equal to the substance that they think they're taking."[154]

If one can "believe" themselves into better health, we really must be Magic. Anthony William is in agreement with the need for positive thoughts and belief for better health. He wants you to practice:

- Holding on to your happy memories, revisiting them to conjure up those warm and fuzzy feelings in the present.
- Finding your voice, expressing your heart, and dreaming of the future, envisioning the career and relationships and abundance that will help you fulfill your purpose.
- Picturing yourself healthy, happy, and healed.
- Finding those moments in the present to be thankful for—even if they're fleeting right now.[155]

He says, "These various forms of light-hearted, optimistic focus are incredibly important steps both for healing and for creating the life you see for yourself."[156]

154 "Dr Joe Dispenza – Official News & Fan Page." 2019. Facebook.Com.
155 William, Anthony. 2017. Medical Medium Thyroid Healing.
156 Ibid.

DIET ON HEALTH

The average diet today is:

- Unnatural
- Highly processed
- Full of artificial sugars
- Tainted with chemicals/toxins/hormones

Dr. David Goff, a heart disease and public health expert at News In Health, explains a study that "establishes the number of … deaths that can be linked to Americans' eating habits, and the number is large."[157] The effects of diet on health has largely gone unnoticed until now. Today, kids as young as their teens are beginning to experience, among other things, some dire problems such as:

- Cancer
- Diabetes
- Autoimmune disease
- Chronic disease
- Addiction
- Mental instability[158]

---

157 "How Your Eating Habits Affect Your Health." 2017. NIH News In Health
158 Ibid.

The health of our gut is, in fact, directly linked to our brain and mental health. Harvard Health says, "A troubled intestine can send signals to the brain, just as a troubled brain can send signals to the gut. Therefore, a person's stomach or intestinal distress can be the cause *or* the product of anxiety, stress, or depression."[159]

We have long been fed myths by food industries in order to keep our money in their pockets—like dairy being needed for strong bones, or meat being the most important source of protein. But humans were not created to drink milk from a cow—we drink milk from our *own* mothers until only a certain age. As for protein, foods like black beans or spinach pack a stronger punch than meat does.

Having "better dietary habits can improve our health quickly," and we can get significant health benefits from:

- Fruits
- Legumes
- Nuts and seeds
- Vegetables
- Water[160]

---

159 Publishing, Harvard. 2019. "The Gut-Brain Connection." Harvard Health
160 "How Your Eating Habits Affect Your Health." 2017. NIH News In Health.

DIET ON ENVIRONMENT

The diet we are accustomed to also contributes to many unacceptable environmental consequences, including, among others:

- Animal torture and abuse
- Environmental degradation
- Water pollution
- High emissions of CO2 and methane

Peta says, "Climate change has been called humankind's greatest challenge and the world's gravest environmental threat … If you're serious about protecting the environment, the most important thing that you can do is stop eating meat, eggs, and dairy products."[161]

Natural, plant-based options are healthier for you, yet also have an indirect beneficial impact on people or environments in other parts of the world which are affected by agri-business. It is important, for the health and well-being of us and our planet, to cut out animal products as well as artificial or processed foods that line the shelves of the supermarket.

You can start small by trying to:

---

161 "Fight Climate Change By Going Vegan." 2019. PETA.

- Make your plate a painting—see how many colors you can fill it with
- Buy local and go to farmer's markets
- Skip the drive-through
- Stick to the produce aisles and buy organic
- Start meatless Mondays
- Eat plant-based

MOVEMENT

Moving our body is critical. Not only does exercising releases endorphins, "chemicals that help to relieve pain or stress, and boost happiness,"[162] but it helps with physical health and even emotional resilience. Tight muscles or painful joints may be the result of past events or emotions that you never fully released or moved on from.

Candance Pert, neuropharmacologist, says, "the *emotional memory is stored in many places in the body, not just or even primarily, in the brain.*"[163] This may be why you feel anxiety in your tight chest, or stress in your clenched jaw or tight neck.

---

162 Berry, Jennifer, and Biggers, Alahna. 2019. "Endorphins: Effects And How To Boost Them." Medical News Today.
163 Lancaster, Heather. 2019. "Top 10 Benefits Of Heart Openers." Yoga-accessories.Com.

When you use physical movement to release tightness or stiffness of your muscles or joints, it can release old emotions for healing. If they stay trapped for too long, they will cause unease and eventually dis-ease in the body. Dr. Susanne Babbel, a psychologist specializing in trauma and depression, says, "Studies have shown that chronic pain might not only be caused by physical injury but also by stress and emotional issues."[164]

One of the most beneficial ways to move our bodies for both our physical and psychological health and regulation is yoga. Yoga is about mind, body, and spirit. My yoga teachers always talk about negativity being stored in the hips.

Through yoga you can come to truly feel and understand what exactly is going on in your body, in your mind, and your emotions. Start small with your movement goals and:

- Wake up in the morning and stretch in your bed
- Touch your toes and feel the rush of your blood
- Take a YouTube yoga class
- If yoga isn't for you, try going for a walk, run, or hike
- If any emotions bubble up, simply feel them and release them

---

164 Mutz, Phil. 2015. "The Incredible Way Your Emotions Are Causing You Physical Pain." Huffpost.Com.

***

Together, the things in this chapter will help you to participate, as well as to feel good *in* your body and *about* your body. They also help you to do your part in understanding and taking care of the planet you live on.

CHAPTER 10:

MENTAL

"Once any person learns the power of his own thoughts, he becomes positive and difficult to subdue."

—NAPOLEON HILL[165]

This chapter will help explain how to gain control of your mind and use it as a force of Magic. The following will teach you to become a magician and to author the story of your own life.

Your thoughts are powerful forces that create your life experience. "Every thought that we build is physical structure that

---

165 Hill, Napoleon, Sharon L Lechter, Mark Victor Hansen, and Michael Bernard Beckwith. 2011. Outwitting The Devil.

comes alive for eternity …" Says Dr. Leaf, neuroscientist.[166] In other words, what you think, you become.

The Scientific American said, "Findings from a new study published in *Cancer* by a Canadian group suggest that our mental state has measurable physical influence on us … " The mind can influence your brain, body, and world.[167]

VOICES IN YOUR HEAD

Most of us have little control over our mind or its contents— there are, at times, bullying voices chattering in your mind. The chattering voices may tell you:

- *You're not good enough.*
- *You are too fat.*
- *You are dumb.*
- *Nobody cares about you.*

Those voices are not you. Those voices belong to your ego, conditioned by past memories, stories, and perceptions. Deepak Chopra explains the ego as our "self-image, not our true self."[168] Napoleon Hill called the ego the Devil.

---

166 Leaf, Dr. 2019. "Deep Cognitive Awareness – Ancient Wisdom Today (Podcast)." Listen Notes.

167 Stetka, Bret. 2019. "Changing Our DNA Through Mind Control?" Scientific American.

168 "What Is Ego? Ask Deepak Chopra!" 2019. Youtube.

Napoleon Hill's so-called Devil says that he will "enter the minds of people through thoughts which they believe to be their own ... fear, superstition, avarice, greed, lust, revenge, anger, vanity, and plain laziness ... "[169]

At times it can be hard to distinguish which voice in your head belongs to your own intuition, benevolently guiding you down the right path. My favorite way to be sure is to question my thoughts:

- *Is this something I would think or say?*
- *Or is this the voice of someone who once hurt me?*
- *Is this the voice of someone I spend a lot of time around?*
- *Is this thought talking down to me?*
- *Does this thought make me feel good or bad?*
- *Is there any truth in this thought at all?*

These practices will help you to become aware of the voices in your head so that you can catch yourself as soon as things start to take a negative turn. Becoming aware of the crowd in your head is the first step to finding *yourself* within it. As you begin to cast out the voices—the internalized external judgements or opinions—your own voice can begin to shine through.

---

169 Hill, Napoleon, Sharon L Lechter, Mark Victor Hansen, and Michael Bernard Beckwith. 2011. Outwitting The Devil.

With more practice distinguishing the sources of your thoughts, it will become easier to listen to your own thoughts, true feelings, and emotions. Once tuned into it, your internal guidance system can then begin to guide you with its full intelligence.

Using your mind in accordance with the *Four Ps of Practical Magic* is a good way to rise above the mental chatter. Remembering and applying the guidelines will help to dispel false voices, as well as intensify focus and clarity upon your own heart and its genuine needs and desires.

FIGHT-OR-FLIGHT

My counselor, Ricardo Contreras, taught me about the prefrontal cortex. This region in the front of the brain controls a person's cognitive abilities such as:

- Rational thinking
- Problem-solving
- Decision making

If in sudden imminent danger, this section of the brain shuts off in order for us to move quickly to safety without rationality getting in the way. Our fear or panic during times of danger is essential. It turns off the logical part of our hardwiring so we can do otherwise dumb things—like jump out of a window to safety, or scream and run for our lives.

Today, we are coming into contact with those type of fight-or-flight situations less and less—we no longer have to live merely in survival mode. However, many of us *are* living in a state of constant or intense stress and anxiety. At a certain level of stress, anger, or anxiety, the prefrontal cortex shuts off and turns on the fight-or-flight response.

If you do not engage in proper stress management, there's a possibility that you could be existing in fight-or-flight mode every day—*with no access to your logical brain.* Not only are you feeling stressed or angry, your rational thinking is quite literally *turned off.*

I used to wonder why I said or did things while frustrated that I later regretted… Now I know why.

In situations where you overheat or over-stress, it takes about *twenty minutes of calm* to re-activate the prefrontal cortex and warm up your logical thinking skills. Our brain requires a break, a time of deep breathing or space from the triggering situation, in order to "reboot."

You see, "the human brain does not know the difference between reality and fiction … In other words, it can't tell the difference between something you're thinking about and something that's actually happening."[170] It cannot tell the difference between the presence of danger and simple anxious thoughts, just as it doesn't know the difference between experienced versus imagined safety. It believes all thoughts to be real.

Simple negative thoughts can gain so much traction and energy that they, alone, may lead to prefrontal cortex slow down or shut-off. Whereas, on the other hand, positive thoughts quite literally make you feel safe. Positivity helps the prefrontal cortex function correctly, and keeps you out of that adrenaline-filled state of survival.

Try to focus on catching yourself when in a dreary train of thought. If you can catch yourself, you can change the narrative you listen to, therefore changing the way you feel and the way you will go on about your day—and your life.

Alternatively, you can practice creative visualization to imagine yourself in the happiest and most safe or peaceful place possible. Immerse yourself in this positive imaginary world, thinking, feeling, and experiencing only good things.

---

170 "The Human Brain Flaw That We All Can Take Advantage Of To Improve Life." 2019. Selfhelpgems.Com.

When caught up in intense negative emotions, you can reclaim your brain by:

- Closing your eyes, taking deep breaths, and focusing on your breathing
- Practicing creative visualization
- Focusing intently on your senses
- Giving yourself good, safe thoughts
- Thinking of five things you are grateful for

These quick, easy practices will help you to gain clarity, calm, and control over your brain. And just like that, you'll be on track to having better cognitive abilities and a healthier mental state.

MENTAL "ILLNESS"

Yes, "illness." I say this because I believe people experiencing mental imbalance are not sick, and that mental illness is often used as a defining term. The "illness" becomes a label and gains power, often becoming intertwined with one's identity.

Being "diagnosed" with a mental illness can make people fearful of themselves, and often leads to years—perhaps a lifetime—on psychological pharmaceuticals. There are

433 million people currently suffering,[171] yet our society has nearly *zero* concept of mental *health*—an epidemic.

According to the World Health Organization there are various factors that contribute to improper mental health:

- Trauma
- Inadequate nutrition
- Stress
- Genetics
- Environmental toxins/hazards
- Living/working conditions[172]

Mental "illness" is caused by many factors. "Illness" may not be much more than coping mechanisms working to preserve a person's sense of safety. These mechanisms may be more intense in a person who has repressed or unresolved emotional or psychological pain or trauma.

One may be battling *intergenerational trauma* which "can leave a chemical mark on a person's genes, which then is passed down to subsequent generations."[173] This is to say that

---

171 "Mental Disorders." 2019. Who.Int.
172 Ibid.
173 Hill, Támara, Annie Vencl, Louie Sandys, and Mubasil Chaudhry. 2019. "How Can Mental Health Professionals Understand Intergenerational Trauma?" ACAMH.

we inherit *mental* illness just as we do *physical* illness. We inherit trauma and unconscious emotional pain.

One may also suffer from *conditioning*—the cycle of passing down learned beliefs. Families learn conditioned behavior and tend to repeat that behavior through generational cycles. If a child grows up around abuse, they too will likely perpetuate abusive behavior.

Beliefs gets passed down endlessly unless one person down the line becomes conscious of the conditioned behavior one is enacting. Once becoming aware of the conditioned behaviors one is living, one can decide to change them and *break the cycle*.

Unprocessed trauma and emotional pain can boil under the surface, manifesting as behavioral complexities that science labels as "symptoms." The dark, heavy connotation that lingers around mental illness makes emotional depth and vulnerability things to be terrified of—nobody wants to risk being labeled as "sick" or "crazy." As we live in fear of not being "normal," we suppress our feelings, which leads back to the bubbling of symptoms—and so the cycle continues.

Nobody should have to walk around with unprocessed trauma, being told they are "simply sick in the head." The problem may not be mental illness, but rather the flawed education and management of true mental health.

Instead of focusing on diagnosing mental problems and pre-scribing chemical band-aids, we should reframe the focus toward maintaining mental health. One should focus on working through wounds and beginning to understand the source of one's pain.

Suffering is an inevitable aspect of being human—we all go through it. We tend to resist it or bury it because it is not pleasant, but suffering brings depth and learning experiences. We must learn how to accept our feelings, good and bad—to process, re-conceptualize, and integrate the thoughts and emotions that come from any suffering we experience.

Vulnerability and honesty with yourself can be scary, but it is a superpower. It leads to more honesty, compassion and genuine connection. Therapy and counseling are amazing ways to become vulnerable in a trusting situation, which allows one to receive validation and support.

Therapy is the new cool thing to do, but it can be scary. If you don't have the nerve to see a therapist yet, you can practice vulnerability by yourself, quietly and safely, by:

- Letting everything out in a private journal, uncensored and free of internal judgement
- Allowing emotions to come up and expressing them in safe ways

- Acknowledging that what you are feeling is natural and valid
- Trying to understand what your thoughts or emotions are communicating to you
- Voice-recording yourself talking things out, then re-listening to gain new perspective
- Giving yourself time and space

METHOD ACTORS

Jim Carrey once said, "As an actor you play characters and then if you go deep enough into those characters you realize that your own character is pretty thin to begin with."[174]

We go through much of our lives role-playing. We have been given:

- Names
- Gender rules
- Religious identities
- Cultural identities
- Nationalities

And we have "clustered them into something that's supposed to be a personality. It doesn't actually exist. None of that stuff

---

174 "The Spiritual Philosophy Of JIM CARREY | Atoms Playing Avatars." 2019. Medium.

if you drill down is real."[175] We are natural method actors from the start, and we can become anything a situation at hand asks.

I noticed one day that when I walked into a classroom, suddenly we were no longer just people. We became students and teacher. Each of us acted, likely unconsciously, according to those specific roles. I then started to notice that same phenomenon *everywhere.*

I realized that within my family, I am not just me, I am a daughter in relation to a parent. At the grocery store, I am no longer me, I am a customer in relation to a cashier. And I had gotten so good at playing these roles, I almost didn't realize they were roles at all.

"Living up to an image that you have of yourself or that other people have of you is inauthentic living," says Eckheart Tolle. "Authentic human interactions become impossible when you lose yourself in a role."[176]

There are certain parts of ourselves that we shut off when in certain situations. There are also aspects of ourselves that only show up when in certain situations. Yet, all the different

175 Ibid.
176 Tolle, Eckhart. 2005. A New Earth. London: Penguin.

faces you present are all still you, and you *can* integrate each varying aspect of your personality.

Try to investigate the roles you play. It takes work and understanding, but it leads to transformation. By befriending the characters you play, you may begin to feel comfortable showing your *true* self in *any* given situation.

Authenticity immediately empowers others to be authentic as well. You are not destined to conform to expectations or stereotypes, though you may be expected to—whether by your family, religion, boss, or social scene. You are alive to be unapologetically you.

There is Magic in that alone. So, learn to drop the roles you play and embody your true self in all situations. You can begin by asking yourself:

- *Am I acting the way I want to, or the way I feel is expected?*
- *What roles do I engage in?*
- *How can I start to step out of those roles?*
- *What would my authentic self be doing?*
- *How can I integrate my authentic self into each role-play situation?*

MENTAL HEALTH → PHYSICAL HEALTH → MENTAL HEALTH

The mind-body connection is everything, as humans are holistic. Physical health comes from mental health, and mental from physical. Tolle expressed that, "Unhappiness or negativity is a disease on our planet. What pollution is on the outer level is negativity on the inner."[177]

Create a healthy, happy future for yourself by thinking productively *now*. With enough time and concentrated effort, your helpful thoughts will become thought-habits, and you will find yourself not only naturally thinking about being healthy, but wanting to take physical steps to ensure that health as well.

If your thoughts repeat, "Health takes too much work," or, "I am too busy to get fit," that is exactly what will come about. You must think healthy thoughts in order to become healthy. However, that doesn't mean you can think, "I am healthy," while eating chips on the couch, then Magically become well.

You can, however, choose to steer your thoughts in a new direction and start inputting thoughts like, "I will feel so good after getting a good sweat in," or, "I am excited to move my body today." With those thoughts in your head, your emotions and actions will start to align, bypassing initial resistance.

---

177 Ibid.

Your body supports you in making healthy decisions by releasing feel-good chemicals like endorphins or serotonin. This helps sustain good thoughts and feelings, which in turn helps you continue to take care of yourself. Your body and your brain work in a continuous feedback loop.

Alternatively, negative thoughts will continue to bring upon physical responses:

- Sweats
- Tummy aches
- Lost appetite
- Migraines
- Nausea

So start to think positively about the state of your physical and mental health. Practice:

- Writing down things you wish you were doing to help yourself
- Thinking about how it would feel to complete these actions
- Feeling this positivity frequently
- Lowering mental resistance

By continually immersing yourself in thoughts of positive actions and feelings so often, you'll release internal resistance and find yourself *wanting* to engage in these behaviors. You will want to experience in reality the good feelings you have been imagining in your head. Becoming physically and mentally healthy can begin as easily as just *thinking about it.*

BRAIN REWIRING

Our brains are *not* hard-wired. They have the ability to change due to neuroplasticity, "the ability of the brain to change continuously throughout an individual's life."[178]

As you now know, our foundations, or bundles of thoughts, are perceived to be the basis of our entire lives. They are learned from our environment and experiences from birth, constructing a platform that we stand on and say, "This is me and my life story." But *you are not your thoughts.*

Yet, your thoughts still have the power to create you and your world. Remember how things only need to repeat three times for it to be remembered? Re-affirming positive statements to yourself is a powerful practice for brain rewiring.

"When you repeatedly align your beliefs, feelings, vision, and actions you will experience lasting changes in your brain."[179]

---

178 "Neuroplasticity." 2019. En.Wikipedia.Org.
179 "5 Ways To Rewire Your Brain For Meaningful Life Changes." 2019. Mindbodygreen.

And the more you repeat thoughts or words to yourself, the more deeply entrenched those thought pathways become in your brain.

There is a crucial need for awareness around the things that you are constantly re-affirming to yourself. By mentally repeating positive statements, goals, or new habits you'd like to embrace, you rewire your brain's pathways. You strengthen your ability to manifest those things in reality, as well as weaken old habits of thought.

You can practice the rewiring process by:

- Making a list of recurring negative thoughts
- Repeatedly saying or thinking their exact opposite
- Writing empowering statements and repeating them each morning
- Envisioning yourself happy, healthy, and loved
- Practicing feeling those positive emotions over and over again

You can practice these from your bed, and literally rewire your brain to give yourself greater potential for a brighter future.

DETACHMENT

Our ego likes to cling to things like:

- People
- Places
- Objects
- Opinions
- Beliefs

We often intertwine our sense of self with the things we are attached to—bundles of thoughts. We cling to them so much that we begin to believe we *are* them. No longer does one say, "I eat a vegan diet," they say, "I am vegan." Just as, "I subscribe to the Catholic religion," becomes, "I am Catholic."

If anybody opposes our opinions, we take it to mean they must not like *us*. Attachment to thought creates conflict within and without. People can fight all day long about why they are right and others are wrong, because being right strengthens your ego, your false sense of self.

I once identified with being vegan. If anybody said veganism was stupid, I would have an emotional response and snap back. *"Have fun being unhealthy and contributing to animal abuse!"* I might've said. At no point in time did that person tell me that I was stupid, yet here I was *fighting* for my sense of self.

Did it truly matter whose point-of-view was *right* here? No—I had to learn that I'm no less of a person because somebody doesn't agree with my eating style. "When you realize it's not personal, there is no longer a compulsion to react as if it were," Tolle wisely stated.[180]

I also realized that the other person's need to be right was an act of *their* ego. And, as Tolle says, "You can only be in a state of non-reaction if you can recognize someone's behavior as coming from the ego."[181]

The idea of detachment is not to stop caring, it is simply to stop confusing *who you are* with *things or thoughts that you have.* You can *believe* in things or *own* things, but those things can never *be you.* Eckhart Tolle says, "You then no longer derive your identity, your sense of who you are, from the incessant stream of thinking that ... you take to be yourself."[182]

Relinquish the idea that any of these labels, identifiers, or stories make up any part of your being. You are so much

180 Tolle, Eckhart. 2005. A New Earth. London: Penguin.
181 Ibid.
182 Ibid.

more than these bundles of thought or belief. Cease the need to always be right, to feel superior, and it will end all forms of violence.

Not only will detachment help you to feel less anger bubbling up on the account of needing to prove yourself, but it may also open you up to different perspectives and new information. It is possible that by detaching yourself from identifications, you may actually deepen your connections to others.

Your ego, or sense of self, is fragile. But *you* are whole, always. Work on detaching yourself from the ego by:

- Making a list of things you identify *with* or *as*—such as "I am Mormon" or "I am rich"
- Ponder on what you would be without those things
- Know that *things* do not add or subtract to your worth as a Magical being
- Practice detachment in your interactions
- Understand that others' reactions are also linked to their egoic attachments
- Try to release negative emotions upon disagreements
- Remember, "This attachment has nothing to do with who I am"

***

These concepts used together will help to shift your Perception and Perspective, allowing you greater control over your mind and actions. As your thoughts and actions come together in harmony, you will be just that much closer to Magically creating the life of your dreams.

CHAPTER 11:

EMOTIONAL

"Rather than being your thoughts and emotions, be the awareness behind them."

—ECKHART TOLLE[183]

Your emotions often go hand-in-hand with your thoughts. When you think of certain people, events, or situations, your body will give physical responses. The reverse can also be true; when you feel a certain way, you might tend to think of certain associations.

---

183 Tolle, Eckhart. 2005. A New Earth. London: Penguin.

This chapter will help you better understand your emotions so that you can use them as the guidance system they are intended to be.

EMOTIONAL REACTIONS AND THE PAIN-BODY

Our emotions are supposed to be our guidance system, yet it can be hard to discern which emotions are true feelings and which are short-lived reactions or temperamental outbursts. The latter type of emotions can be monsters if you have little awareness of them.

Emotional reactions can largely cloud our judgement. When we feel very strongly this way or that way, we tend to make quick, thoughtless decisions based upon those feelings.

I have learned by now that if I am feeling a burst of anger, the thoughts and actions that I take from that state may not be the smartest. If I am feeling sudden fear, it's likely that I either sabotage myself or get completely paralyzed. I now know that it is extremely important to not let emotional reactions lead my thoughts, therefore directing my actions.

Reactive emotions stem from the ego—the part of you that gets attached to thought. Each time your thinking is clouded by plumes of emotion, the ego grows stronger. These short-lived emotions like to do the talking and acting *for* you, before you get the chance to settle and think things over.

What's more, negative emotions can also linger within you over time, patiently waiting for a chance to re-emerge and gain more power. They use more emotional reactions to keep them alive.

Tolle called these lingering negative emotions the "pain-body"—"an addiction to unhappiness."[184] In an interview with *Science Of Mind*, he said the pain-body "periodically becomes activated, and when it does, it seeks more suffering to feed on."[185]

I'm sure you have felt this ... I know I have. There have been times that I have been so pissed off, I did not want to feel happier, but rather wished to inflict that same pain onto others. I wanted others to feel just as mad as I did, and their anger went on to feed my own pain-body even more.

There are various ways to feed and strengthen the pain-body:

- Negative thinking
- Negative experiences

---

184 Ibid.
185 Juline, Kathy. 2019. Eckharttolletv.Com.

- Drama in interactions
- Complaining
- Blaming

Tolle teaches about the pain-body, "Once you recognize it, it cannot take over your mind, feed on your negative thoughts, and control your internal dialogue as well as what you say and do."[186] It can at times be a struggle telling the difference between the feelings that are from you, and those that are generated from the pain-body's knee-jerk reactions, though.

Eckhart Tolle suggests, "Rather than being your thoughts and emotions, be the awareness behind them."[187] You can practice this awareness by:

- Observing your emotional reactions
- Letting yourself feel the emotions that arise within you, and not pushing any away
- Investigating if there is something these emotions can communicate to you
- Waiting until the emotion decreases in intensity to take any action

---

186 Ibid.
187 Tolle, Eckhart. 2005. A New Earth. London: Penguin.

Chances are, the bad emotions fizzle down a bit once you've given yourself time and space to observe them. Instead of acting those emotions out, you have now gained awareness of them and they've lost their grip on you. You also now have an opportunity to learn from them.

You can then begin to ask questions to your emotional reactions:

- *Why are you feeling this way?*
- *What are you stemming from?*
- *What can I do to make you feel better?*

Ask them whatever you please. Your feelings can then flow through you, being felt and acknowledged, and then pass. Do whatever you need to release negative emotions in a healthy way.

Soon you will have returned to your own zero state, with new knowledge about yourself and your feelings. Cultivating awareness of emotional reactions is an act of self-love and compassion.

COMMUNICATION VERSUS COMPREHENSION

It can be hard to communicate exactly what we feel to people, which is a major cause of emotional reactions. We may be fearful of being vulnerable, or simply not have the words to accurately express ourselves. On the other hand, people can only comprehend what they are *ready* to understand.

Communication also goes through numerous filters between sender and receiver, like:

- Opinions
- Experiences
- Education
- Values
- Stereotypes[188]

Both speaker and listener have preconceived notions, past memories, and other things that the message is filtered through. Even physical noise in the room can obstruct a message from getting through correctly.

Language itself can be a huge barrier to understanding and comprehension. Our words and feelings when passed on to others largely get broken down and lose meaning. You also have a lens which may keep you from understanding clearly.

Frustration, anger, and impatience can arise when you try to communicate and are not fully understood. A lot of

---

188 Sharpe, Dave. 2019. "Effective Communication." Msucommunitydevelopment.Org.

misunderstandings fly under the radar, but there are some cases of misunderstanding that stick out like a sore thumb. It can feel personal, and your mood may change like the flick of a switch.

Some things I have caught myself thinking during miscommunications are:

- *How could you possibly think that's what I meant?*
- *Are you even listening to me?*
- *I swear, you never pay attention to me!*
- *Are you deaf or just stupid?*

Communication is one thing, comprehension is another. Know that during times of miscommunication or misunderstanding, the street goes two ways and just about anything could've interrupted the flow.

When misunderstandings arise remember that this is, unfortunately, the nature of language. A misunderstanding should not be a cause for anger, blame, or disappointment. Do not let the pitfalls of communication be the reason the pain-body gets activated and starts to burn you.

Know that you likely misunderstand others, as they do you. It is OK to be confused—when it happens, laugh. It is also OK to ask questions in order to deepen comprehension and connection. When one can understand that communication is easily flawed, one can also lose the personal emotional reactions that come with misunderstanding.

EMOTIONAL AWARENESS

Trying to discern genuine feelings from short-sighted emotions can feel like walking a tightrope. Your pain-body likes to be in control. If that tightrope walk takes too much mental effort, it is easy to slip away and let it take over.

Emotional reactions are the equivalent of being "possessed" by emotion. The emotions likely did the talking while your authentic self sat in the background, unaware it had been compromised. One of the most beneficial things you can do for yourself and those around you is to cultivate awareness surrounding your emotions.

Tolle explained that "disidentification from the emotion and just being in the now moment is the way to stop the cycle of constantly recreating painful experiences."[189] Acknowledging an emotion rather than becoming the emotion can help keep you grounded in the moment, with a calm and collected inner state. There are ways to cultivate awareness of your emotions, for example:

---

189 Juline, Kathy. 2019. Eckharttolletv.Com.

- Stopping to ask if your reaction is justified, or an overreaction
- Contemplating if acting on that emotion would turn into an outburst you might regret
- Noticing if you are quick to engage in arguments and spats
- Practicing sitting with negative emotions before responding or making decisions

Your pain-body lives as a parasite does—draining you in order to sustain itself. It begins within as a slow bubble, until it gets so aggravated that it boils over the surface and burns you. It burns others as well, but the most damage is done to yourself.

I once heard the idea that holding onto anger is like grasping a hot coal with the intention of burning somebody else. In truth, holding onto and therefore prolonging *any* negative emotional reaction is like squeezing that same hot coal.

Once you can meet the bubbling emotions inside of you with non-judgmental awareness, the bubbles will subside and the waters within you can calm down. They will return to their original state, smooth and flowing, and the pain-body will die down as it gets less fuel.

Along with this awareness, you can choose to do some investigation. You can learn the workings behind the emotional reaction and become more aware of it for the future:

- Think about what it was that triggered your emotional reaction
- What about it was triggering, and why?
- How might your pain-body respond to that trigger?
- How can your heart choose to respond instead?

When you feel overcome with emotion, breathe. Do not act or react. Try to focus on nothing but your senses and the steady stream of breath flowing in through your nose, and back out again.

You might notice your breathing is fast and shallow. Perhaps you have forgotten to breathe entirely. Try to slow down and deepen your breathing, paying attention to nothing but the innnn … and the outtttt.

Take stock of yourself after a few breaths:

- Are you still feeling as intensely?
- Do you still wish to respond or react the way you did before breathing?

- Do you feel like your initial emotional reaction was greater than was necessary?
- Do you still feel that initial emotion *at all*?

Awareness of emotions is the best way to understand what it is we are feeling and why. It is the way to take our power back from emotions, using them as a guide rather than being controlled by them.

FEELING EMOTIONS

All of your emotions are valid and they are important; they simply should not control you. It is very important that you *let yourself feel your emotions*—that you do not shy away from them, close them in, bottle them up, or pretend they do not exist. Expressing your emotions is a healthy thing to do, in productive ways:

- When *joyful*, laugh and smile, sing or dance, and have fun sharing it with others
- If *angry*, try to break a sweat, give yourself a time out, or write an angry letter and rip it to shreds
- During *sadness*, give yourself comfort, cry, ask for support or talk to someone you trust
- When *fear* is in your way, go for a walk in nature, get support and perspective from others, or practice a mindfulness meditation

- When overcome with *love*, shower yourself with it, express it to those you feel it for, and give support to those who may need it
- If you're *unsure* of your feelings, write freely in a journal, read back over it as a learning experience, and do not seek to label your feelings too quickly

It is important to let your emotions run their course, and there are healthy ways to express all emotions, good or bad.

REPRESSED EMOTION → ANXIETY

An emotion is a certain type of energy that we feel—it can drain us or hype us up. When we feel an emotion, we should always take action to properly let it out.

Many of us tend to repress our emotions, but it comes at a cost. A study on the consequences of repressed emotions states that "emotional status has a direct and profound influence on physical and mental health."[190]

In a different study, "One group of ninety subjects was instructed to control and hide their feelings. The other was

---

190 Patel, Jainish, and Prittesh Patel. 2019. "Consequences Of Repression Of Emotion: Physical Health, Mental Health And General Well Being." International Journal Of Psychotherapy Practice And Research

allowed to express them freely … The study's most interesting finding was the physiological response in the suppression group … In short, the suppression group was undergoing panic and anxiety!"[191]

And this included panic and anxiety from the suppression of *positive emotions* as well. It seems that the energy of any type of emotion can have a direct impact on the state of our brain and body. Feeling anxious may not be anxiety at all, but the bubbling of a different emotion we are not taking proper care to express.

"Whatever the reason, many of us deny ourselves feelings of natural joy and happiness. Unexplained anxiety, and particularly panic, is often an indication of such unexpressed emotion."[192] I know that I have had times where I have repressed positive emotions because I didn't want to seem too happy, or because I felt awkward to be the only person showing excitement.

One time I was in a meeting with a professor when I *finally* got a text I had been waiting for. And it was worth celebration! But there was nothing I could say or do about it at the time.

---

191 Siegel, Dr. Yaakov. 2016. "Do We Suppress Positive Emotion?" Nefesh. Org.
192 Ibid.

I then went to classes, forgot about the text and about the excitement I had been unable to unleash. Anxious feelings began brewing later on that day, but I absolutely could not pinpoint any source of anxiety.

With more investigation, I realized that I was feeling anxious because I still had pent up energy inside of me waiting to burst over that text! Realizing this, I was then able to properly celebrate and dance around, which extinguished any feelings of anxiety within me.

Other feelings that I've noticed can ramp up my heart rate or energy levels are fear or anger, as well as more positive emotions like surprise. It is important to express *all* of these emotions, to get your body back to its equilibrium. Ask yourself:

- "Why might I be feeling anxious?
- "Are these true feelings of anxiety?"
- "Or might I just have bottled up emotions inside me?"
- "What emotions, positive or negative, have I not properly expressed?"

No emotion is bad or wrong. All deserve their rightful expression in whatever form feels right to the person feeling them. They must be expressed in order to keep your mind and body feeling good.

LOVE > FEAR

I don't believe the opposite of love is hate, but rather that hate is just one of the many symptoms or byproducts of fear. I believe that fear is love's opposite—but that love and fear are two sides of the same coin. One cannot exist without knowing the other.

The intersection of love and fear brings way for special things like bravery and courage. One cannot be brave without first being afraid, nor can one be courageous without love trumping their fear.

Jim Folk overcame his anxiety disorder and has been living anxiety-free for twenty-seven years. Folk wrote that, "Fear is a thought process that triggers the fight-or-flight response. Fear and anxiety are caused by how we THINK. In this sense, fear and anxiety are not real but only imagined … This means we can overcome fear and anxiety by learning to think differently."[193]

In order to think differently, one must first cultivate awareness, which we have already been practicing. Do not be afraid of fear, as it only consists of thoughts. Do not take it to be real, daunting or controlling.

---

193 Folk, Jim. 2019. "What Is The Best Way To Overcome Anxiety Disorder?" Anxietycentre.Com.

Napoleon Hill said, "Fear is the tool of a man-made devil. Self-confident faith in one's self is both the man-made weapon which defeats this devil and the man-made tool which builds a triumphant life ... It is a link to the irresistible forces of the universe which stand behind a man who does not believe in failure and defeat as being anything but temporary experiences."[194]

Fear is only necessary in survival situations, which we are now mostly free of. Instead, fear can be used as your signposts. You can look at fear from a higher perspective to see it differently and to learn from it. Candice Wu, holistic psychologist and intuitive coach says, "Fear is love and energy in disguise."[195]

Wu tells a story of a client of hers who was afraid to move somewhere new. Instead of busting down that wall of fear with force, Wu asked her client to honor that the wall had a message for her. Once the client asked her fear what message it held, she began crying—a realization that she gave too much to others and not herself.

The client learned that she was not scared of moving, but of feeling the guilt associated with making a choice for herself.

---

194 Hill, Napoleon, Sharon L Lechter, Mark Victor Hansen, and Michael Bernard Beckwith. 2011. Outwitting The Devil.
195 Wu, Candice. 2019. "Fear Is Love And Energy In Disguise: What To Do When Fear Creeps In." Candicewu.Com.

Now that she understood the message behind her fear, she was able to freely give to herself, and to move forward with her life in her own way. Just like that, her fear dissipated.[196]

You can learn to feel the fear, learn from it, and do the scary thing anyways. Do hurdles with fear. Jump over fear to get to the love that waits on the other side. Each hurdle you conquer will teach you about yourself, empower you, and cultivate self-love and compassion

By using fear as your guideline, the hurdles will become easier to jump as you go, until you find fear hardly existing. Then you may find yourself living in a world of endless possibilities, in which you can create your life exactly the way you imagine, without psyching yourself out.

Napoleon Hill expressed that he wished people "would learn the greatest of all truths—that the time they spend in fearing something would, if reversed, give them all they want in the material world."[197]

So ask yourself, "What would I do if I wasn't afraid?"

Then do exactly that.

---

196 Ibid.
197 Hill, Napoleon, Sharon L Lechter, Mark Victor Hansen, and Michael Bernard Beckwith. 2011. Outwitting The Devil.

SELF-LOVE AND SELF-CARE

For many, the terms self-love or self-care probably brings up ideas such as eating a tub of ice cream, binging Netflix, or drinking your own bottle of wine—"Treat yourself," right?

But self-care doesn't mean binging when you feel down. Self-love is taking good care of your needs over anybody else's, without feeling guilty about it. *You* are the objective of your life—nobody else.

I have known the feeling of giving so much love, energy and effort to others but getting so little in return. At times where I felt drained or exhausted, I wished somebody would love me the way I am able and willing to love them.

Here's the thing: Somebody *can* love me that way—*myself.* We should all love ourselves to pieces, guilt-free. *You* always come first.

It's not always easy, especially given the amount of negative self-talk that you likely live with inside of your head. It is easy to hate on yourself, to think that you're not good enough, and to compare yourself to others.

But *only you* can love yourself exactly the way you need to be loved. It is an inside job. Nobody can ever fix you or make you better—most people likely haven't figured out how to heal themselves, so how would you expect them to do any better for you?

So fix yourself. Or, rather, *heal* yourself. Remember that love is the most powerful healing force there is.

Along with the process of loving yourself comes learning to be alone, and genuinely enjoying it. There is a huge difference between being alone and being lonely, yet it can feel like walking a fine line. You are always with yourself, so you might as well enjoy the person you're spending so much time with.

It can definitely be hard at first and during certain times, but there is a special kind of freedom and exhilaration that comes from learning to do things on your own terms, like:

- Growing at your own pace
- Making all your own decisions
- Changing direction without guilt or burden
- Adapting and evolving however you please

To learn to be alone is to learn to love. You can never be able to truly give love to anyone else until you learn to love YOU for who you are. You have to fill your own cup with love before it can spill into others' lives.

Start treating yourself the way you wish you were treated.
Imagine the way you'd treat your best friend, or your significant other. Treat yourself that way. Do things like:

- Buy yourself flowers
- Take yourself on dates
- Hype yourself up in the mirror
- Have fun with yourself and crack jokes
- Meet your every need
- Kiss your wounds

I sometimes imagine that I am my soulmate, meeting *me* for the first time. I think about *all* the things this soulmate would absolutely love about me. Sometimes I just mentally compliment myself, other times I write those things down so I can come back later and remember all the little things that make me *Magic*.

***

Together, these bits of advice will help you gain awareness of your emotions so as to not let them take control of you. They may lead you to a deeper understanding of your inner workings, and lead you to new hidden insights that may have been repressed or masked.

CHAPTER 12:

 SPIRITUAL

"No human being need fear the Devil, or worry about how to flatter God."

—NAPOLEON HILL[198]

This chapter is about taking your power and potential back from any external sources, and beginning to understand true spirituality versus religious dogma. I hope to help you understand and love yourself as the incredible, infinite, Magical spirit that you truly are.

My religion never quite helped me understand spirituality, but rather taught me (indirectly) to fear God and "His"

---

198 Hill, Napoleon, Sharon L Lechter, Mark Victor Hansen, and Michael Bernard Beckwith. 2011. Outwitting The Devil.

judgement. (I put quotations around "His" because I am unsure why we have labeled the most powerful force in the universe with a human gender.) When fearing your creator, yet being told that you are made in "His" image, you begin to judge and fear yourself as well—at least, I did.

Hill said, "The highest power in the universe can be used for constructive purposes, through what you call God, or it can be used for negative purposes, through what you call the Devil. And something more important still, it can be used by any human being just as effectively as by God or the Devil."[199]

SPIRITUALITY VERSUS RELIGION VERSUS SCIENCE

One does not need to subscribe to a religion to connect with their spirituality, or the inner and outer Magic that surrounds and fills us all. Spirituality does *not* need to be synonymous with religion, but they both focus on the invisible. Alternatively, science reveres materialism and tends to dismiss things unseen.

"Phenomena that are not physical, measurable, or provable from scientific observations, are assumed to be unreal … Hundreds of years ago, electricity, radiation, and radio waves

───────────────

199 Ibid.

were not something that people believed in, and if described, these ideas would have been considered preposterous and impossible," said Gordon in The *Secret Nature of Matter*.[200]

I knew there had to be a connecting point for all three—a way for them to coexist without butting heads. Amazingly enough, science, in its effort to discover what material existence is made of, traveled so deeply that it discovered *visible reality is actually composed of the invisible*. It has unveiled the quantum, energetic, spiritual world talked about in religious books.

God is said to be omnipotent (all powerful), omnipresent (all present), and omniscient (all knowing). And as Shaman Durek says in his podcast *Ancient Wisdom Today*, "If you were to take science and push it up against religion, the first thing science would do is to find words that correlate with mathematical principles ... If you take the word 'omni' and move it into a mathematical principle that we can understand in science, it means quantum."[201]

Dr. Leaf, neuroscientist, then chimes in to talk about the spiritual findings of quantum physics. Just as I explained how emotions have a vibrational frequency, she says, "There's

200 Gordon, Richard. 2017. Secret Nature Of Matter.
201 Durek, Shaman, and Dr. Leaf. 2019. "Deep Cognitive Awareness." Listen Notes.

a whole group of scientists that are outstandingly brilliant and they are showing that we as humanity are made of love-waves. We, literally, are waves of love and we're immersed in love, and there is mathematical and quantum calculations showing the beauty of it … "[202]

This scientific explanation finally made sense to me about "God," an all-loving creator of life. Richard Gordon mirrors Dr. Leaf's words, saying, "Love is the primary carrier wave of life-force energy. Love is the universal frequency which is able to communicate to all beings … "[203] As we are made from love, so do we have the power and responsibility to *choose* love.

Dr. Leaf powerfully explains, "Quantum physics shows this causality, it shows how we are the pinnacle of God's creation, and quantum physics cannot exist without humanity's ability to think, feel, and choose … If you actually read the Bible, or read any ancient text, there's a huge responsibility we have as humans to … activate this potential within us … So as we think, feel, and choose, we are accessing the wisdom of the ancients … We are accessing God's wisdom … We are accessing the waves of love-energy in the quantum fields … "[204]

---

202 Ibid.
203 Gordon, Richard. 2017. Secret Nature Of Matter.
204 Durek, Shaman, and Dr. Leaf. 2019. "Deep Cognitive Awareness." Listen Notes.

When you *choose* to live rooted into a place of love, you can:

- Live in greater emotional and spiritual alignment
- Tap into your full potential
- Align yourself with the love-waves that surround us
- Input much-needed love into a struggling world

Dr. Leaf continues, "And it's not just impacting us, brain, soul, and body, it's affecting generations to come ... We have this potential within us to access this God-ness. If we are made in God's image, then that means at our core we are perfect ... We are these incredibly powerful beings with the ability to create."[205]

Mind you, *this is a neuroscientist talking about God in scientific terms that directly correlate to ancient religious texts.* We have a powerful opportunity to choose to be loving in every thought and action, therefore choosing to live life for something greater than just ourselves. We simply have the ability to choose otherwise.

But as Gordon says, "There is power in love. This power can forever change you, and change the world."[206]

---

205 Ibid.
206 Gordon, Richard. 2017. Secret Nature Of Matter.

"SIN"

The concept of "sinning" is something taught by a lot of religious systems. Elder L. Tom Perry, a member of the Quorum of the Twelve Apostles of The LDS church, states that "there are moral absolutes. Sin will always be sin. Disobedience to the Lord's commandments will always deprive us of His blessings."[207] The Catholic Church states, "Sin is an offense against God."[208]

To commit a sin has become something people initially feel afraid of, or, if enacted, ashamed of. Yet, Tolle teaches that, "Sin is a word that has been greatly misunderstood and misinterpreted. Literally translated from the ancient Greek in which the New Testament was written, to sin means to miss the mark, as an archer who misses the target, so to sin means to *miss the point* of human existence. It means to live unskillfully, blindly, and thus to suffer and cause suffering."[209]

We have long been taught that life is a game of good versus evil, but I believe there is no such thing as sin, only an absence of love. Free will—an act of love in itself—gives us the power to choose whether we will dwell in love or slip into more negative emotions and states of being and experiencing.

207 "LDS Quotations". 2019. Ldsquotations.Com
208 "Catechism Of The Catholic Church – Sin." 2019. Vatican.Va.
209 Tolle, Eckhart. 2005. A New Earth. London: Penguin.

For "sin" should not be a concept that keeps you terrified of your own nature, instilled with fear of wrong-doing, or of judgement by an all-mighty force. Life is to be experienced in its fullness.

Hill said that, "Sin is anything one does or thinks which causes one to be unhappy! Human beings who are in sound physical and spiritual health should be at peace with themselves and always happy. Any form of mental or physical misery indicates the presence of sin."[210]

To sin, or to miss the point, is to:

- Continue to live beneath the static of the world
- Live without seeing the deeper meaning in what you do with this experience here on Earth
- Forget the loving truth, the complete Magic, of who and what you are
- Live in a place of suffering, or unhappiness
- Act out of alignment with love

Reaching to please an external God is absolutely unnecessary. What truly matters is that you look into *your own heart* and let it guide you to what you love. As they say, "The kingdom of God is within you."

---

210 Hill, Napoleon, Sharon L Lechter, Mark Victor Hansen, and Michael Bernard Beckwith. 2011. Outwitting The Devil.

Instead of making decisions based on what would be pleasing to God, try looking at things and deciding "yes" or "no" based on what pleases *you*. Say yes to what you excites you, say no to the things that do not. Ask yourself:

- *What and who do I love?*
- *What makes me happy?*
- *If I could do anything in the world, what would it be?*
- *How can I cultivate more of my own happiness?*
- *What things am I doing that I actually dislike?*

We get to choose our state of mind every second of every day, and we *can* choose to do only the things we love. Yet, it can still be hard to do. Luckily, there are methods to help us connect to our inner spirituality, our inner "love-ness" or "God-ness," in Dr. Leaf's words, which I will go into now.

PRESENCE

To connect to your inner "love-ness," you must become present. You must begin witnessing the moment you are living in and being truly alive. Presence simply means being *here, now.*

Tolle teaches, "Always say 'yes' to the present moment. What could be more futile, more insane, than to create inner resistance to what already is? What could be more insane than to oppose life itself, which is now and always now? Surrender to what is. Say 'yes' to life—and see how life suddenly starts working for you rather than against you."[211]

When you *choose* a moment, giving it your alert attention and full presence, you are extending the fullest form of love. People feel loved when they are paid attention to—when they are chosen by you as part of the present moment. "When the other person realizes that his or her presence has been recognized and confirmed, he or she will blossom like a flower. To be loved is to be recognized as existing."[212]

It is in these times of presence that the subtle guidance of your heart and soul can present itself most clearly. Your mind can cease to be a barrier between you, the infinite nature of your soul and the world around you. Presence can allow:

- Intuition to come out to play, nudging you toward things you love
- Lessons to pop out of seemingly insignificant things
- A deeper sense of understanding and appreciation to emerge

You can transcend thought and become present to the moment by engaging the five senses, as in:

---

211 Tolle, Eckhart. 2005. A New Earth. London: Penguin.
212 Nhat Hanh, Thich. 2019. "You Are Here." Google Books.

- Listening intently to your surroundings
- Seeing and noticing small details
- Tasting what's currently on your tongue
- Smelling the scent of the space you're in
- Feeling different textures around you

I would love for you to go ahead and practice that list now, before moving on.

MEDITATION

Meditation is a spiritual act and mental workout that allows you to declutter and get back to that place of love that dwells within you. It is "a process where you attune your physical mind and body to its spiritual source."[213]

During meditation, our thoughts might wander and day-dream. Meditation helps to become aware of those thoughts, the ultimate practice of presence. It is a time for:

- Awareness of thought
- Zero-action
- Being alone with yourself
- Experiencing what lies within and around you

---

213 "Meditation | Inward Journey." 2019. Inwardjourney.Com.

"I don't have time to meditate," you think. Whoa! How did I know exactly what you were thinking? Because that's what my brain automatically reverts to as well. But just think ... how many ten minute breaks do you take each day on social media?

Still, sitting silently doing nothing for an excess of ten minutes can feel like a huge sacrifice to make with a busy schedule. It seems almost paradoxical, for how can you get anything done by focusing on nothing?

Scientifically, meditation allows you to reprogram yourself. According to Headspace, a great guided meditation app, simply sitting and becoming aware of your thoughts and breath will help:

- Increase your ability to be compassionate
- Decrease stress levels
- Reduce aggression and irritability
- Improve focus
- Increase overall happiness[214]

As one consistently meditates, the brain is literally re-wired to function from that place of peace and intense presence—even during chaotic times. "Normally the neural pathways from the bodily sensation and fear centers of the brain ... are really

---

214 "Researching Meditation And Mindfulness – Headspace." 2019. Headspace.

strong. When we meditate, we weaken this neural connection … So when we experience scary or upsetting sensations, we can more easily look at them rationally."[215]

Our brains are often so cluttered and dampened by activity that we are unaware of the spirit, consciousness, awareness, or Magic that lies beyond it. When we give ourselves space to breathe and not to think, we are more easily able to tap into that field of infinite Magic and potential—the universal observer, the quantum waves of love.

Meditation allows us to receive divine insight that we otherwise may not come into contact with, buried under the ego. Some things that help my with my own meditation practices are:

- Sacrificing one social media check, replacing it with meditation
- Sitting alone, closing my eyes, and focusing on my breathing
- Deepening my breath, or witnessing its natural rhythm
- Noticing my thoughts, seeing if I can catch them as they enter my brain
- Doing guided meditations if I want to focus on a specific subject (the Insight Timer app is my favorite)

---

215 Stillman, Jessica. 2019. "Neuroscience: This Is How Meditation Changes Your Brain For The Better."

BREATH

A Sanskrit proverb reads, "For breath is life, and if you breathe well you will live long on earth."[216] Our breath is an important, yet often overlooked, connecting point for mind and body.

Sheila Patel, M.D., says, "The mind, body, and breath are intimately connected and can influence each other. Our breathing is influenced by our thoughts, and our thoughts and physiology can be influenced by our breath."[217] Breathing itself is a huge health benefit, but it goes beyond physical or mental health.

Thich Nhat Hanh, a Vietnamese monk, teaches, "There are those of us who are alive but don't know it. But when you breathe in, and you are aware of your in-breath, you touch the miracle of being alive."[218] If you can remember your breath, a deep and constant in and out, it will translate into an understanding of Patterns and Reflections.

You can learn from your breath the need for in and out, up and down, fullness and emptiness. As you learn to surf the waves of the breath that sustains itself, you can take the

---

216 "Breathing For Life: The Mind-Body Healing Benefits Of Pranayama." 2019. The Chopra Center.
217 Ibid.
218 Hanh, Thich. 2019. "Thich Nhat Hanh On The Practice Of Mindfulness." Lion's Roar.

breath's profound lessons and apply them to your life. And when things crash down, you can surrender with excitement to do it all again.

I practice connecting to my own breath by:

- Breathing in, breathing out
- Going from shallow chest-breathing, to breathing deep in my belly
- Noticing my belly's subtle rise and fall
- Sending my breath to different places in my body, filling it or stretching it
- Thanking my breath for keeping me alive, even when it's the last thing on my mind

SLEEP, DREAMS, AND HEALING

Sleep is an act of self-love, one of the most spiritual acts we can take part in. It also happens naturally, every single night, *and* it is free. Yet, many of us deprive ourselves of this luxury.

While we sleep, our bodies rest and heal. According to Anthony William, "10 p.m. to 2 a.m. is a sacred window. It's the time at night when your body does most of its healing. If you are able to sleep during that period, your body is healing at an accelerated rate."[219]

Dreams are also a source of healing for the soul, just as sleep is healing to the body. Our dreams are an easy way to access our subconscious mind and our spirit. It can be one of the quickest paths to what lies within us beneath the surface, often hidden from our conscious thinking mind.

Anthony William explains dream-healing, saying, "When we are wounded, a physical component in the brain puts up a barrier to prevent us from constantly processing and reprocessing the pain, so that we can be productive and move forward during our waking hours ... When we're not conscious, the emotional walls come down so the soul can do its cleanup and repair work ... through our dreams. If this didn't happen, frustration, anger, fear, betrayal, guilt, and humiliation would build up and up and up within us until they overpowered the strength of the walls holding them in place and took over our waking lives."[220]

He calls it "nightly house-cleaning" that helps us face our suffering without becoming scarred by it. He explains that bad dreams work to our benefit, helping to remind us of

219 William, Anthony. 2017. Medical Medium Thyroid Healing.
220 Ibid.

things that may need some attention so we can fully process it and move on.

As it turns out, even nightmares are our friends: Adelita Chirino, a psychotherapist and spiritual counselor, says, "The biggest thing is to know, as most good dream teachers will say, that dreams come in the service of our best interests, just the way good friends do. If they've resorted to scaring us, well they've got a good reason for doing it that way."[221]

BEYOND JUST DREAMING

Chirino uses her dreams as a method of learning. She says, "For me the best answers come from my dreams and what they've taught me ... Our Native American ancestors knew that dreams tell us the secret wishes of our soul."[222]

Dreams have been the source of many creations. Paul McCartney said about the song *Yesterday*, "I woke up one morning with a tune in my head and I thought, 'Hey, I don't know this tune—or do I?' ... I went to the piano and found the chords to it, made sure I remembered it and then hawked it round to all my friends, asking what it was: 'Do

---

221 Chirino, Adelita. 2019. "Lita Dreaming." Litadreaming.Blogspot. Com
222 Ibid.

you know this? It's a good little tune, but I couldn't have written it because I dreamt it.'"[223]

Dreams can hold:

- Memories
- Subconscious beliefs
- Divine inspiration
- Precognitive or prophetic aspects
- Connection to those who have passed on
- Symbolism from the collective unconscious, the invisible web of energy that entangles us all[224]

Dreaming can also take a turn toward the deeply spiritual, as in lucid dreaming—the ability to become "awake" within a dream, understanding that your body is still asleep. Becoming lucid within dreams is an old spiritual practice. The more aware one can become inside of a dream, the more aware they can become during waking life, and vice versa.

"Tibetan Dream Yoga is the original form of lucid dreaming documented for at least 1,000 years … The initial aim is to

---

223 Gregoire, Caroly. 2017. "8 Famous Ideas That Came From Dreams (Literally)." Huffpost.Com.
224 Chirino, Adelita. 2019. "Lita Dreaming." Litadreaming.Blogspot. Com.

awaken the consciousness in the dream state."[225] They practice until they are pros—able to travel to different worlds or shape-shift into different creatures by will.

Lucid dreams also give insight into how powerfully creative our thoughts truly are—bad thoughts can give way to nightmares, good thoughts allow Magical, creative, and transcendent experiences. "Director Christopher Nolan took the inspiration for his 2010 psychological thriller *Inception* from his own lucid dreams."[226]

To receive spiritual, creative insight from dreams, as well as gain sufficient awareness to try lucid dreaming, begin by:

- Writing down your dreams as soon as you wake up
- Give yourself reality checks—how do you *know* you're awake?
- Pay attention to the feelings that linger within you after waking
- Start paying attention to symbolism—perhaps pick up a dream dictionary
- Ask what the dream means—if you already have a theory, pay attention to that intuition, as it's probably correct

---

225 Turner, Rebecca. 2019. "Dream Yoga: Lucid Dreaming In Tibetan Buddhism." World-Of-Lucid-Dreaming.Com.
226 Gregoire, Caroly. 2017. "8 Famous Ideas That Came From Dreams (Literally)." Huffpost.Com

RESONANCE

Like vibration attracts like vibration, like a magnet. Paying attention to what it is that you are drawn to and resonate with is an awesome way to connect to your intuition and find what it has to teach you about yourself. Notice what you notice, whether it be:

- People
- Music
- Clothes
- Quotes
- Movies
- Books

Your outer world is a reflection of your inner world. That is to say, you find things that you are searching for—whether consciously or unconsciously. You know you're deeply resonating with something if:

- It gives you a feeling of relief or peace
- It perfectly matches your current feelings or mood
- Goosebumps or thrill-bumps rise up on your arms or body
- You wish to pass it on to/share it with somebody else
- It invokes an emotional response

Those could all be considered spiritual experiences. You are connecting with something on a deep, internal level. When you feel recognition or connection, take the time to ponder *why*.

Every person is at their own stage in life, walking a path of unique hopes, dreams, and desires. Your feelings change as your world shifts, you learn lessons, and your heart continues to guide you. One thing that strikes your heart today may be totally not relatable tomorrow or next week.

You can make connections or take inspiration from anywhere, anyone, or anything. You can also grow to feel disconnected to something you used to deeply resonate with. You do not need to explain to others why your preferences may change, just pay attention to yourself and what the things you resonate with are telling you.

GRATITUDE = ABUNDANCE

Gratitude is the ultimate form of love—a gift that should always be given if felt, and never held onto. According to Harvard Health, "Gratitude helps people feel more positive emotions, relish good experiences, improve their health, deal with adversity, and build strong relationships."[227]

---

227 Publishing, Harvard. 2019. "Giving Thanks Can Make You Happier." Harvard Health.

When you rise into a space of gratitude, you are painting a picture of the beauty in your life. It is a way to shine light on the big things, as well as the small things that often get overlooked. It takes into account every little thing that plays a role in your life that has helped you or changed you in any way.

"Gratitude unlocks the fullness of life. It turns what we have into enough, and more. It turns denial into acceptance, chaos into order, confusion into clarity. It can turn a meal into a feast, a house into a home, a stranger into a friend," said Melody Beattie, a self-help author.[228]

And when you tune your mind to gratefulness, it becomes easier to spot the good things. Knowing what you have, and how lucky and blessed you are to have it, sends out a wonderful surge of energy into your environment and will bring love and beauty right back to you. Stephen Richards, another self-help author, says, "Gratitude also opens your eyes to the limitless potential of the universe, while dissatisfaction closes your eyes to it."[229]

In a state of gratitude, you are acting from your heart. Your thoughts and actions can come into loving alignment and the negative things start to fall away. It takes your perspective

---

228 Martinez, Dr. Nikki. 2019. "73 Gratitude Quotes Celebrating Life, Love & Friends". Everyday Power.
229 Ibid.

from the complaint of not having or being enough, and shifts it to feeling fullness.

Taking time to acknowledge and build gratitude will open you up to the good things in life, as well as invite more abundance your way. Start slow:

- Begin each day with gratitude—you can write it down, think it, or say it out loud
- If you can express your gratitude directly to who or what you're grateful for, do it
- Do guided meditations on gratitude
- Visualize sending love and appreciation out around you, as if you were telepathic

Look for the things that have done you well in any way, and hold a place for them in your heart, even if only for a moment.

***

Together, these practices can help you tune into the spiritual presence that lies beneath your thoughts and emotions. They can give you a sense of peace and wholeness within you that has likely been mostly undiscovered until now, as well as open you up to the mystical force that you may call "God," "source," "the universe," or "Magic." Each practice helps you become more strongly unified with your heart and intuition.

CONCLUSION:

"The story ... is now in your hands. The benefits you will receive from it will be in exact proportion to the thought it inspires in you ... you need not agree with every portion of it. You have only to think and to reach your own conclusions concerning every part of it. How reasonable that is."

—NAPOLEON HILL[230]

You have successfully inspected my filing cabinet of thoughts and feelings. All the things that have weighed on my mind and heart are now in your hands for you to do with them what you please.

---

230 Hill, Napoleon, Sharon L Lechter, Mark Victor Hansen, and Michael Bernard Beckwith. 2011. Outwitting The Devil.

That you've made it to the conclusion of this book can mean only one thing: You are a vibrational match with what this book has to share. Therefore, you are an essential part of the shifting of mass consciousness and awakening of the world to the Magic that supports us.

This world is teeming with Magic, if only you attune yourself to see and feel it. Magic can rebuild foundations, heal trauma, rewrite brain and body chemistry, and even speak to you through what some call the "inner voice" or intuition. You are a powerful being who also has the ability to create Magic, within yourself as well as in the world around you.

Though our brains largely mold by the age of five according to our environments, Magic can help shift your perceptions to give you a stronger, healthier foundation. Magic can guide you intelligently from within when you feel lost, hopeless, or confused.

Books largely collect Magic, to live long past the authors who created it, and that book Magic blesses the lives of the readers who give presence to their words. Other authors who match the vibration you are wishing for can guide you during low times, as well. You can find Magic in the words of the people who inspire you.

Investing in a more Magical perception of yourself in this life can promote you from the main character up to the author of your life story. You can use this authorial Magic to write yourself a happier narrative, doing good for your community and planet as a result. The Magic of writing our own dream stories will help to give a new direction to the existing storylines, shifting them from hatred, judgement, and division to peace, connection, and compassion.

You, as a mostly invisible being, are capable of tuning into Magic on so many different levels. You can work Magic into your physical health, become Magically understanding of your emotions, Magically rewire your brain, as well as tap into the infinite spiritual Magic that exists as deep within you as it does far beyond you.

The universe is always using Magic, playing around with things constantly winking in and out of existence—nature going from birth to death to rebirth. It leaves us hints of its creative, controlled power through patterns, cycles, waves, connections, and reflections. This Magic responds to you like a magnet, bringing to you whatever you are intent on. This Magic is always creating opportunities for you to empower yourself.

When you finally begin to recognize the power and beauty in real-life Magic, and start to use it on behalf of your heart, it steps in to lend you a helping hand. And I hope that by reading this book, you will have learned how to both better recognize and better utilize this Magic within the world and yourself. I hope you will empower yourself to embrace it and use it to change your own life.

I hope you find the Magic contained within this book that resonates with you personally, and use it to formulate a new life-practice that works for you. As you begin to align your thoughts, emotions, and actions with your heart's Magical guidance, you will build yourself a sturdier foundation from which you can develop your dream self and life.

Have more fun.
Be more selfish.
Listen to your intuition.
Love the present moment.
Make life happen *for* you, not *to* you.

Make your own Magic.

APPENDIX

INTRODUCTION:

"Facts & Statistics | Anxiety And Depression Association Of America, ADAA." 2019. *Adaa.Org.* https://adaa.org/about-adaa/press-room/facts-statistics.

Hill, Napoleon, Sharon L Lechter, Mark Victor Hansen, and Michael Bernard Beckwith. 2011. Outwitting The Devil.

Parr, Ben. 2019. "Google: There Are 129,864,880 Books In The Entire World". *Mashable.* https://mashable.com/2010/08/05/number-of-books-in-the-world/.

"The American Foundation For Suicide Prevention: (Year 2017)". 2019. *AFSP.* https://afsp.org/cdc-2017/.

CHAPTER 1:

"Abraham Maslow." 2019. En.Wikipedia.Org. https://en.wikipedia.org/wiki/Abraham_Maslow

"Abraham Maslow Quote." 2019. A-Z Quotes. https://www.azquotes.com/quote/652384.

"Abraham Maslow's Hierarchy Of Needs." 2019. Medium. https://medium.com/@elskenneymedia/abraham-maslows-hierarchy-of-needs-cc1bc0124a24.

"Brain Development – First Things First." 2019. First Things First. https://www.firstthingsfirst.org/early-childhood-matters/brain-development/.

"Brain Pathways, Explained." 2019. Youtube. https://www.youtube.com/watch?v=poLEYYyJo-E.

"Definition Of Foundation." 2019. Merriam-Webster.Com. https://www.merriam-webster.com/dictionary/foundation.

Lepera, Nicole. 2019. "Things You'll Learn On A Healing Journey." Pictame.Com. https://www.pictame.com/media/2103807407930043058_7822041710.

Mcleod, Saul. 2019. "Maslow's Hierarchy Of Needs." Simply Psychology. https://www.simplypsychology.org/maslow. html.

Nunley, Kathie. 2019. "Dr. Kathie Nunley's Layered Curriculum Web Site For Educators". Help4teachers.Com. http://help4teachers.com/interdisciplinary.htm.

"Parents, Let's Talk About Maslow's Hierarchy Of Needs – Bluedollarbull". 2019. Bluedollarbull. https://bluedollarbull.com/maslows-hierarchy-of-needs/.

"Synchronicity". 2019. En.Wikipedia.Org. https://en.wikipedia. org/wiki/Synchronicity.

"Timothy Leary Quote." 2019. Quotefancy.Com. https://quotefancy.com/quote/1002486/Timothy-Leary-The-brain-is-not-a-blind-reactive-machine-but-a-complex-sensitive.

Tolle, Eckhart. 2016. A New Earth. London: Penguin.

CHAPTER 2:

Hatch, Heidi. 2019. "Utah Youth Suicide Now Leading Cause Of Death For Utah Kids Ages 11-17." KUTV. http://kutv. com/news/local/utah-youth-suicide-now-leading-cause-of-death-for-utah-kids-ages-11-17.

Hickman, Luke. 2019. "Why It's Really Called Happy Valley – ." Uvureview.Com. https://www.uvureview.com/recent/artsculture/whyitsreallycalledhappyvalley/.

"Op-Ed: Responding To Ellen On Mormons And Teen Suicide." 2019. Deseret News. https://www.deseret.com/2018/6/14/20647036/op-ed-responding-to-ellen-on-mormons-and-teen-suicide.

Runnells, Jeremy. 2017. "CES Letter." Cesletter.Org. https://cesletter.org/ces-letter.html.

Stauffer, McKenzie. 2019. "Provo Named Least Diverse City In America." KUTV. https://kutv.com/news/local/provo-named-least-diverse-city-in-america.

"Temple Recommend Interview Questions". 2019. Mormonthink.Com. http://www.mormonthink.com/glossary/templerecommend.htm.

"The Church Of Jesus Christ Of Latter-Day Saints." 2019. Churchofjesuschrist.Org. https://www.churchofjesuschrist.org/?lang=eng.

"The Money Behind The Mormon Message." 2012. The Salt Lake Tribune. https://archive.sltrib.com/article.php?id=54478720&itype=CMSID.

CHAPTER 3:

Burnett, Frances Hodgson. 2000. The Secret Garden. South Bend: Infomotions, Inc.

Gordon, Richard. 2017. The Secret Nature Of Matter.

Hill, Napoleon, Sharon L Lechter, Mark Victor Hansen, and Michael Bernard Beckwith. 2011. Outwitting The Devil.

Quinn, Daniel. 1992. Ishmael.

"Readishmael.Com – Ishmael By Daniel Quinn Wins Ted Turner's Tomorrow Fellowship". 2019. Readishmael.Com. http://www.readishmael.com/readishturner.html.

"Richard Gordon". 2019. Amazon.Com. https://www.amazon.com/Richard-G ordon/e/B0045AMF0E%3Fref=dbs_a_mng_rwt_scns_share.

Tolle, Eckhart. 1997. The Power Of Now.

William, Anthony. 2017. Medical Medium Thyroid Healing.

CHAPTER 4:

Braden, Gregg. 2000. "The Isaiah Effect." Google Books.

"Buddha On Truth.". 2019. Spiritualityhealth.Com. https://spiritualityhealth.com/quotes/three-things-cannot-be-long-hidden-sun-moon-and.

Dispenza, Joe. 2017. "Becoming Supernatural." Google Books.

Dossey, Larry. 2016. "Pseudoscience Versus Science." Physics Today 69 (11): 10-10. doi:10.1063/pt.3.3343.

Gordon, Richard. 2017. Secret Nature Of Matter.

Hill, Napoleon, Sharon L Lechter, Mark Victor Hansen, and Michael Bernard Beckwith. 2011. Outwitting The Devil.

Sturm, Rudiger. 2019. "Jim Carrey | The Talks." The Talks. https://the-talks.com/interview/jim-carrey/.

CHAPTER 5:

"Ancient History". 2019. En.M.Wikipedia.Org. https://en.m.wikipedia.org/wiki/Ancient_history.

Annabelle Timsit, Annalisa Merelli. 2019. "For 10 Years, Students In Texas Have Used A Textbook That Says Not All Slaves Were Unhappy." Quartz.

"'First Human' Discovered In Ethiopia." 2019. BBC News. https://www.bbc.co.uk/news/science-environ-ment-31718336.

Gordon, Richard. 2017. Secret Nature Of Matter.

Hill, Napoleon, Sharon L Lechter, Mark Victor Hansen, and Michael Bernard Beckwith. 2011. Outwitting The Devil.

Hsu, Jeremy. 2019. "The Hard Truth About The Rhino Horn &Ldquo;Aphrodisiac&Rdquo; Market." Scientific American. https://www.scientificamerican.com/article/the-hard-truth-about-the-rhino-horn-aphrodisiac-market/.

"Human Overpopulation." 2019. En.Wikipedia.Org. https://en.wikipedia.org/wiki/Human_overpopulation.

Quinn, Daniel. 1992. Ishmael.

Roser, Max, Hannah Ritchie, and Esteban Ortiz-Ospina. 2019. "World Population Growth." Our World In Data. https://ourworldindata.org/world-population-growth.

"World Population Clock: 7.7 Billion People (2019) – Worldometers." 2019. Worldometers.Info. https://www.worldometers.info/world-population/.

CHAPTER 6:

"Disability And Health." 2019. Who.Int. https://www.who.int/news-room/fact-sheets/detail/disability-and-health.

Gordon, Richard. 2017. Secret Nature Of Matter.

Quinn, Daniel. 1992. Ishmael.

"Steven Hassan's BITE Model – Freedom Of Mind Resource Center." 2019. Freedom Of Mind Resource Center. https://freedomofmind.com/bite-model/.

Tolle, Eckhart. 2005. A New Earth. London: Penguin.

"What Is Effective Frequency? Definition And Meaning." 2019. Businessdictionary.Com. http://www.businessdictionary.com/definition/effective-frequency.html I.

"Wild Earth News & Facts By World Animal Foundation." 2019. Worldanimalfoundation.Com. https://www.worldanimalfoundation.com/advocate/wild-earth/.

"WHO | Mental Disorders Affect One In Four People." 2019. Who.Int. https://www.who.int/whr/2001/media_centre/press_release/en/.

Zoë Schlanger, Daniel Wolfe. 2019. "Fires In The Amazon Rainforests Were Likely Intentional." Quartz. https://qz.com/1692804/fires-in-the-amazon-rainforests-were-likely-intentional/.

CHAPTER 7:

"Abraham-Hicks". 2019. Facebook.Com. https://www.facebook.com/Abraham.Hicks/posts/start-telling-a-better-feeling-story-about-the-things-that-are-important-to-you-/533556600104333/.

"Alan Watts How To Stop Being Self Conscious". 2019. Youtube. https://www.youtube.com/watch?v=DOED4FIDlq4.

Bridges, Lawrence. 2019. "A Conversation With Ray Bradbury." Youtube. https://www.youtube.com/watch?v=P-F3uZf4G3Lo&t=311s.

Childre, Doc. 2019. "Renewing Heart Qualities." https://www.heartmath.com/blog/articles/renewing-heart-qualities-by-doc-childre/.

Contributor, Tim. 2019. "Right Again, Einstein! Wobbling Pulsar Confirms General Relativity." Livescience.Com. https://www.livescience.com/wobbling-pulsar-confirms-einstein.html.

Gordon, Richard. 2017. Secret Nature Of Matter.

Hill, Napoleon, Sharon L Lechter, Mark Victor Hansen, and Michael Bernard Beckwith. 2011. Outwitting The Devil.

"Here's How Many Iphones Are Currently Being Used World-wide." 2019. Fortune. https://fortune.com/2017/03/06/apple-iphone-use-worldwide/.

Juma, Norbert. 2019. "60 Buddha Quotes About Life, Death, Peace, And Love." Everyday Power. https://everydaypower.com/buddha-quotes-on-love/.

LePera, Nicole. 2019. "The Holistic Psychologist – The Power To Heal Yourself". The Holistic Psychologist. https://yourholisticpsychologist.com.

"'Selfie' Named As Word Of The Year". 2019. BBC News. https://www.bbc.com/news/uk-24992393.

"Steve Jobs' 2005 Stanford Commencement Address." 2019. Forbes.Com. https://www.forbes.com/sites/davide-walt/2011/10/05/steve-jobs-2005-stanford-commence-ment-address/#1efd94745852.

"The Science Of Heartmath." 2019. https://www.heartmath.com/science/.

Tolle, Eckhart. 2005. A New Earth. London: Penguin.

Umoh, Ruth. 2019. "Steve Jobs And Albert Einstein Both Attributed Their Extraordinary Success To This Personality Trait." CNBC. https://www.cnbc.com/2017/06/29/steve-jobs-and-albert-einstein-both-attributed-their-extraordinary-success-to-this-personality-trait.html.

"Why Elon Musk Thinks We're Already Cyborgs". 2019. Big Think. https://bigthink.com/paul-r atner/why-elon-musk-thinks-we-are-already-cyborgs.

CHAPTER 8:

"20 Amazing Facts About The Human Body". 2019. The Guardian. https://www.theguardian.com/science/2013/jan/27/20-human-body-facts-science.

"Abraham Hicks You Are Always Manifesting." 2019. Pinterest. https://www.pinterest.co.uk/pin/660551470317321237/?nic=1.

Emerson, Ralph Waldo. 2019. "The Law Of Compensation." Briantracy.Com. https://www.briantracy.com/blog/personal-success/the-law-of-compensation/.

Hill, Napoleon, Sharon L Lechter, Mark Victor Hansen, and Michael Bernard Beckwith. 2011. Outwitting The Devil.

Staff, Gaia. 2018. "As Above So Below; Alchemy And The Emerald Tablet | Gaia". Gaia. https://www.gaia.com/article/emerald-tablet-101-the-birth-of-alchemy.

CHAPTER 9:

Berry, Jennifer, and Biggers, Alahna. 2019. "Endorphins: Effects And How To Boost Them." Medical News Today. https://www.medicalnewstoday.com/articles/320839.php.

"Birth Control Pills: General Information." 2019. Center For Young Women's Health. https://youngwomenshealth.org/2013/07/25/birth-control-pills/.

Chevalier, Gaétan, Stephen T. Sinatra, James L. Oschman, Karol Sokal, and Pawel Sokal. 2012. "Earthing: Health Implications Of Reconnecting The Human Body To The Earth's Surface Electrons." Journal Of Environmental And Public Health

"Dr Joe Dispenza – OFFICIAL NEWS & FAN PAGE." 2019. Facebook.Com. https://www.facebook.com/DrJoeDispenzaOfficialNewsFanPage/posts/i-started-becoming-fascinated-with-the-idea-that-you-can-give-someone-a-sugar-pi/3500370469988322/.

Drywater-Whitekiller, Virginia. 2019. "We Belong To The Land: Native Americans Experiencing And Coping With Racial Microagressions". Questia.Com. https://www.questia.com/library/journal/1P4-1956424557/we-be-long-to-the-land-native-americans-experiencing.

Electronics, Valley. 2019. "Technology – This Is How Daysy Works. Natural Ovulation Tracking." Usa.Daysy.Me. https://usa.daysy.me/technology/.

"Fight Climate Change By Going Vegan." 2019. PETA. https://www.peta.org/issues/animals-used-for-food/glob-al-warming/.

"FREQUENTLY ASKED QUESTIONS." 2019. Plastic Pollu-tion Coalition. https://www.plasticpollutioncoalition.org/survey-focus-and-approach-1.

Groth, Aimee. 2019. "You're The Average Of The Five Peo-ple You Spend The Most Time With." Business Insider. https://www.businessinsider.com/jim-rohn-youre-the-average-of-the-five-people-you-spend-the-most-time-with-2012-7.

Hill, Napoleon, Sharon L Lechter, Mark Victor Hansen, and Michael Bernard Beckwith. 2011. Outwitting The Devil.

"How Your Eating Habits Affect Your Health." 2017. NIH News In Health. https://newsinhealth.nih.gov/2017/05/how-your-eating-habits-affect-your-health.

"Ideas To Try In Nature." 2019. Mind.Org.Uk. https://www.mind.org.uk/information-support/tips-for-everyday-living/nature-and-mental-health/ideas-to-try-in-nature/#.XYPfuS2ZOt8.

Klein, Marty. 2019. "Science Shows What Sexual Repression Actually Looks Like". Psychology Today. https://www.psychologytoday.com/us/blog/sexual-intelligence/201011/science-shows-what-sexual-repression-actually-looks.

Lancaster, Heather. 2019. "Top 10 Benefits Of Heart Openers." Yogaaccessories.Com. https://www.yogaaccessories.com/top-10-benefits-of-heart-openers.

Mo, Matty. 2019. "War & Porn: Becoming An Avatar." Medium. https://medium.com/@themostfamousartist/war-porn-a-story-of-matty-mo-5f95a151e27c.

Mutz, Phil. 2015. "The Incredible Way Your Emotions Are Causing You Physical Pain." Huffpost.Com. https://

www.huffpost.com/entry/the-incredible-way-your-e_b_7464472.

"Nature And Mental Health." 2019. Mind.Org.Uk. https://www.mind.org.uk/information-support/tips-for-everyday-living/nature-and-mental-health/#.XYPdGS2ZOt8.

"Plastic Threatens Our Health From Before Production To Long After It'S Thrown Away: Report." 2019. EHN. https://www.ehn.org/plastic-pollution-and-human-health-2629322391.html.

Publishing, Harvard. 2019. "The Power Of The Placebo Effect." Harvard Health. https://www.health.harvard.edu/mental-health/the-power-of-the-placebo-effect.

Tello, Monique. 2016. "Can Hormonal Birth Control Trigger Depression?." Harvard Health Blog. https://www.health.harvard.edu/blog/can-hormonal-birth-control-trigger-depression-2016101710514.

van den Bosch, Matilda. 2017. "Natural Environments, Health, And Well-Being." Oxford Research Encyclopedia.

"What Is A Vasectomy?." 2019. Urologyhealth.Org. https://www.urologyhealth.org/urologic-conditions/vasectomy.

William, Anthony. 2017. Medical Medium Thyroid Healing.

CHAPTER 10:

"5 Ways To Rewire Your Brain For Meaningful Life Changes." 2019. Mindbodygreen. https://www.mindbodygreen. com/0-11762/5-ways-to-rewire-your-brain-for-meaningful-life-changes.html.

Hill, Napoleon, Sharon L Lechter, Mark Victor Hansen, and Michael Bernard Beckwith. 2011. Outwitting The Devil.

Leaf, Dr. 2019. "Deep Cognitive Awareness – Ancient Wisdom Today (Podcast)." Listen Notes. https://www.listennotes. com/podcasts/ancient-wisdom-today/cxxvii-deep-cognitive-fFoGQEmAwWy/

"Mental Disorders." 2019. Who.Int. https://www.who.int/ news-room/fact-sheets/detail/mental-disorders.

Stetka, Bret. 2019. "Changing Our DNA Through Mind Control?." Scientific American. https://www.scientificamerican.com/article/changing-our-dna-through-mind-control/.

"The Human Brain Flaw That We All Can Take Advantage Of To Improve Life." 2019. Selfhelpgems.Com. http://www. selfhelpgems.com/human-brain-flaw/.

"The Spiritual Philosophy Of JIM CARREY | Atoms Playing Avatars." 2019. Medium. https://medium.com/the-mission/jim-carrey-atoms-playing-avatars-5cf3db20a390.

Tolle, Eckhart. 2005. A New Earth. London: Penguin.

"What Is Ego? Ask Deepak Chopra!." 2019. Youtube. https:// www.youtube.com/watch?v=dehu27Uo2xk.

CHAPTER 11:

Folk, Jim. 2019. "What Is The Best Way To Overcome Anxiety Disorder?." Anxietycentre.Com. https://www.anxietycentre.com/anxiety/treatment/best-way-to-overcome-anxiety-disorder.shtml.

Juline, Kathy. 2019. Eckharttolletv.Com. http://www.eckharttolletv.com/article/Awakening-Your-Spiritual-Lifes-Purpose

Patel, Jainish, and Prittesh Patel. 2019. "Consequences Of Repression Of Emotion: Physical Health, Mental Health And General Well Being." International Journal Of Psychotherapy Practice And Research 1 (3): 16-21. doi:10.14302/issn.2574-612x.ijpr-18-2564.

Sharpe, Dave. 2019. "Effective Communication." Msucommunitydevelopment.Org. Accessed September 21. http://www.msucommunitydevelopment.org/effectivecommunication.html.

Siegel, Dr. Yaakov. 2016. "Do We Suppress Positive Emotion?." Nefesh.Org. https://nefesh.org/drsiegel/do-we-suppress-positive-emotion/read.

Tolle, Eckhart. 2005. A New Earth. London: Penguin.

Wu, Candice. 2019. "Fear Is Love And Energy In Disguise: What To Do When Fear Creeps In." Candicewu.Com. https://candicewu.com/fear-is-love-and-energy-in-disguise-what-to-do-when-fear-creeps-in/.

CHAPTER 12:

"Breathing For Life: The Mind-Body Healing Benefits Of Pranayama." 2019. The Chopra Center.

Chirino, Adelita. 2019. "Lita Dreaming." Litadreaming.Blogspot.Com. http://litadreaming.blogspot.com/2010/.

Durek, Shaman, and Dr. Leaf. 2019. "Deep Cognitive Awareness." Listen Notes. https://www.listennotes.com/podcasts/ancient-wisdom-today/cxxvii-deep-cognitive-fFoGQEmAwWy/.

Gordon, Richard. 2017. Secret Nature Of Matter.

Gregoire, Caroly. 2017. "8 Famous Ideas That Came From Dreams (Literally)." Huffpost.Com. https://www.huffpost.com/entry/famous-ideas-from-dreams_n_4276838.

Hanh, Thich. 2019. "Thich Nhat Hanh On The Practice Of Mindfulness." Lion's Roar. https://www.lionsroar.com/mindful-living-thich-nhat-hanh-on-the-practice-of-mindfulness-march-2010/.

Hill, Napoleon, Sharon L Lechter, Mark Victor Hansen, and Michael Bernard Beckwith. 2011. Outwitting The Devil.

"LDS Quotations." 2019. Ldsquotations.Com. https://www.ldsquotations.com/quote/topic/1412.

Martinez, Dr. Nikki. 2019. "73 Gratitude Quotes Celebrating Life, Love & Friends." Everyday Power. https://everyday-power.com/gratitude-quotes/.

"Meditation | Inward Journey." 2019. Inwardjourney.Com. http://www.inwardjourney.com/tools/meditation/.

Nhat Hanh, Thich. 2019. "You Are Here." Google Books. https://books.google.com/books?id=CxOP-

Publishing, Harvard. 2019. "Giving Thanks Can Make You Happier." Harvard Health.

Stillman, Jessica. 2019. "Neuroscience: This Is How Meditation Changes Your Brain For The Better."

Tolle, Eckhart. 2005. A New Earth. London: Penguin.

Turner, Rebecca. 2019. "Dream Yoga: Lucid Dreaming In Tibetan Buddhism." World-Of-Lucid-Dreaming.Com.

William, Anthony. 2017. Medical Medium Thyroid Healing.

ACKNOWLEDGEMENTS

Setting out on a journey to fill a book cover-to-cover with inspiration takes time, effort, and an incredible amount of help. This journey took me higher and lower than I had ever been before. Words cannot accurately describe the gratitude I feel for the people who offered a helping hand along the way, but I will do my best to put it into writing.

Firstly, the most special thanks goes out to my sweet, self-less parents for taking care of me like a child again while I was writing this book. Second off, thank you to Eric Koester for creating this book program, Brian Bies for blessing us all with the best energy during weekly meetings, and New Degree Press for publishing me. Thirdly, thanks to my editors Kirk Schueler and Maylon Gardner for helping me condense my sporadic thoughts into something publishable, as well as

Kayla Lefevre for copyediting. The last special thanks goes out to Odera Nkem-Mmekam, Lawrence Kajura, Sam Lynch, and Antonio Banos for understanding my ideas and helping them come to life.

And thank you to everyone who:pre-ordered the eBook, paperback, and multiple copies to make publishing and an audiobook possible, helped spread the word about *Make Your Own Magic* to gather amazing momentum, and helped me publish a book I am proud of. I am sincerely grateful for all of your help.

Eric Koester
Ryan Hatch
Odera Nkem-Mmekam
Tracy Palica*
Shannon Morrison
Garrett Clark
Kylie Darger
Jakub Swierczynski
Eleni Wilding
Jeannie Fillmore
Stephen Schmutz Jr
Mason Tucker
Matt Hill
Eric N Graham*
Eileen Stremming

Grant Williams
Lita Childers*
Camren Hansen
Braden Frampton
Howard Pae*
Robert Barker
Zak Callahan
Antonio Drouet
Logan Kamer
Simoné Marshall-Smith
Elizabeth Sundeen
Zack Andersen*
Alaina Krayeski
Aaron Galindo
Grant Just

Nick Martineau

Grant Dunn

Jane Rhodes*

Jake Fauglid

Danette Fish

Natasha Jelly

Cody Fisher

Shelby Elliot

Stacy Palica

Robert Boone IV

Carolina Wuergler

Kassi York

Alexandra Loosigian

Jennifer Shin*

Mike and Jeanette Higel

Parker Goodwin

Jason Fanaika

Dusty Crocker

Samuel Lynch

Alexis Schrepple*

Sophia Edwards

Jillian Rosadino

Trevor Schulz

Antonio Banos

Ashley Coles

Shelby Russell

Kevin Swiss*

Griffin Germond

Kami Reiser

Ashley English

Kaylene Palica

Tyler Metcalfe

Kyle Howard

McKinley Vaughan

Amanda Diaz

Ethan Bush

Irene Valentina Tejera Mossi

Andrew Wilding

Jennifer House

Mike Stroshine

Sadie Nelson

Ryan Poelman*

Al Vargas

Juan-Luc Durant

Melanie Christensen

Britney Pannell

Milan Cook

Wayne Palica*

Key: *multiple copies/campaign contributions